"Why is it important to affirm a child? Because a child who is truly accepted by his parents ... can grow up learning to accept himself. .... He'll be able to admit his own failures and weaknesses. He'll be able to forget himself and love others.

"See yourself as God sees you: a little child of eternity, moldable and piiable.... Surrender yourself totally under His hands. ... Let there be no more masking, posturing, faking on your part. ... (Thus) the generations meet each other's needs ... and revival, renewal, become your constant, ever-fresh way of life."

Children Are Wet Cement will teach you how to both discipline and disciple a child. You'll find projects ... Bible study ... plenty of personal illustrations ... and specific examples of positive ways to raise children, from handling the toddler to letting the mature child go. Anne Ortlund's compassionate, humorous, and candid guidance will comfort and encourage you as you care for the children in your life.

ANNE ORTLUND

CHILDREN ARE WET CEMENT

AN AUTHORS GUILD BACKINPRINT.COM EDITION

Children Are Wet Cement

All Rights Reserved © 1997, 2002 by Anne Ortlund

No part of this book may be reproduced or transmitted in any form
or by any means, graphic, electronic, or mechanical, including photocopying,
recording, taping, or by any information storage or retrieval system,
without the permission in writing from the publisher.

AN AUTHORS GUILD BACKINPRINT.COM EDITION

Published by iUniverse, Inc.

For information address:
iUniverse, Inc.
5220 S. 16th St., Suite 200
Lincoln, NE 68512
www.iuniverse.com

Originally published by Fleming H. Revell

Scripture quotations are from the HOLY BIBLE, NEW INTERNATIONAL
VERSION ®. NIV ®. Copyright © 1973, 1978, 1984 by International Bible Society.
Used by permission of Zondervan Publishing House. All rights reserved.

Quotations by Sally Folger Dye are from *To Put Down or Build Up*, Summer
Institute of Linguistics, Papua, New Guinea, 1979.

ISBN: 0-595-22663-9

Printed in the United States of America

To our eight grandchildren
this book is affectionately dedicated:

Mindy Harrah
Beth Anne Harrah
Lisa McClure
Laurie McClure
John McClure IV
Eric Ortlund
Krista Ortlund
Dane Ortlund

"It's a book about handling children," I was telling Sherry.

Sherry said, "Mom, do you suppose you would let me write the Foreword?"

"Dear Sherry!" I said. "You're my firstborn. What could be more appropriate? Write whatever you want." How could I know she was going to undercut me with snide remarks about burnt toast?

Foreword

I was "wet cement," and some footprints that made forever impressions on my life belong to Anne Ortlund, the author of this book and my mother.

When you think of the childhood memories your mother created for you, you may well think of the smell of fresh-baked bread and your mom in the kitchen providing good things for the family. Believe me, I have no memories like that of my mother. I used to wake up to the sound of the burnt part being scraped off the toast. I don't think my mother ever baked bread in her life, and quite frankly, she wasn't a very good cook. *(Sh-h-h! Don't tell her I said that!)*

But the impressions left on my life by my mother are lots better than memories of fresh-baked bread. I remember her as a growing, learning, changing person.

Remember the days when the body of Christ had the notion that pastors and their wives had to be perfect? Well, not really perfect—but pastors and their wives had to run a close second to Jesus in sinlessness. And if, God forbid, the pastor's wife really was human, she sure didn't let anyone else know about it.

I remember my mother's discovering that to really love the Church and become involved in people's lives she must become vulnerable, a person dependent on God's grace for forgiveness. Mom was, and still is, a growing person.

How did that imprint my life? It gave me hope. I don't have

to have all the answers by the time I'm thirty-three years old or forty or whatever. I know that God will continue to change me, and hopefully, my two daughters will be left with the impression of a mother who learns and changes—and admits it.

Probably the most important legacy I received from my parents was a frequently heard challenge: "Be big for God. Go for it. Don't settle for less than God's best." My parents often said to their children, "We don't care what you do for a living; you can dig ditches with our blessing; but oh, accomplish big things for God. Be fanatical Christians. Love God with all you've got."

My mother wasn't a great cook, but my mother—and my father, too—were great at loving Jesus. That's a terrific inheritance.

I pray that through this book my mother will place her imprint on your life as she has on mine.

SHERRY HARRAH
(Anne's daughter)

Contents

Section I

About Me ...

1

Children are wet cement.

I was, too, as a child.

The summer I was two and a half, we went camping in Minnesota—Daddy, Mother, six-year-old Bobby, and I. I was little Betty Ann Sweet then, and I hated to get up then as I do now. Every morning I could hear the family packing up to leave, with Daddy chanting loudly for my benefit, "I want my clothes, I want my clothes! I want to get up, I want to get up!"

I didn't, and I wouldn't, so eventually down would come the little pup tent on top of me. I got up.

I'm grateful to Daddy, now in heaven, for that memory. It made a distinct impression on me, Betty Ann Sweet, wet cement: that Daddy was fun and preferred a light touch to teach me cooperation—but after the fun, *he would win, and I would cooperate.*

Do you doubt my remembering such early details? For years my mother doubted this memory of mine. "Anne," she'd say, "you're just remembering what you've heard us talking about."

Then one day when I was college age, she and I were shopping together, and I said, "Mother, look at that china over there! That's the same pattern we had when we lived in Wichita."

Well, the fact is, we moved away from both Wichita and the china when I was two and a half. After that my mother didn't question my remembering things.

Daddy was a young U.S. Army lieutenant, and the move took us to Fort Benning, Georgia, where the big girl in the quarters next to ours taught me to swing cats around by their tails. I did it with her, and for a while I did it furtively without her. My, they did yowl!

She also told me horrible ghost stories. When she told me the Red Hands were after me, I ran and walked several miles, before I was finally picked up by Daddy, out searching for me in the car. For a long time afterward I thought the Red Hands were all around—like under my bed—and I would take a running leap to get into it at night, so the Red Hands wouldn't grab me.

Yes, I was wet cement.

I felt terrific at age four, when I put on my favorite dress, a pale-green dotted swiss Mother had made me (with white lace around the neck). When I had it on, I dreamt I was really gorgeous, and that everyone was looking at me, admiring me.

Then there was the big maid who told me if I wasn't good, she'd stuff me into the garbage can. I worried about that for a long time.

For some reason, I had a constipation problem. Every morning, Daddy and I sat in the bathroom together, me perched on the throne in earnest concentration, while he held my two hands inside his big ones and shared my concern. That is a tender memory.

Mother put plenty of starch and spunk into us kids; we all inherited it. She was the one who rebuked us and spanked us and saw that we shaped up. The Lord knows we needed it all! And so we have rebuked and spanked liberally the next generation. Daddy's only punishment of me was the hurt in his voice when he would say, "Anne! Be nice!"—truly disappointed when I wasn't up to his expectations.

I still long to be "nice," so that he'll be only delighted when I see him next in eternity.

Mother and Daddy sang a lot of silly songs together, especially riding along in our Essex. I remember "Nothing could be finer than to be in Carolina in the mo-o-o-orning. . . ." And Daddy sang serious love songs to Mother—while she played the piano—songs like "Sing me to sleep; Love, you alone/Seem to be left me for my own. . . ."

Of two things in life we children were certain: that the earth was solid, and that Daddy loved Mother.

On summer evenings in Georgia, there was no going to bed in the heat. So our parents would give Bobby and me our baths, dress us in our pajamas, and put us into the back of the Essex. During the long drives we'd fall asleep, and get carried into the house to bed.

The Commanding Officer of Fort Benning at the time was Colonel George Marshall, later to be General Marshall, who became one of our most distinguished Secretaries of State and father of the Marshall Plan. When a Commanding Officer came with his wife to pay a social call, you didn't apologize for anything; everything was to be perfect, and your Army career might be determined by it.

When Colonel and Mrs. Marshall came to call at our house, my parents were in bed with the worst kind of flu. They sprang out of bed to groom themselves perfectly in minimum time, and sent me out to the living room, meanwhile, to keep the Marshalls entertained. I charmed them by telling in detail my parents' every physical symptom, and every recent incident related to their flu. General Marshall reminded Daddy of it every time he saw him for years—fortunately laughing.

One Christmas Daddy and Mother made plans for us to travel clear to California to vacation with his brothers and sisters. As we stood on the train platform and this enormous black monster arrived, chugging and roaring and belching, I screamed almost louder than the train, trembling all over, the tears dripping off my face. I would *not* get on! Eventually, because of schedule, Daddy simply carried me on anyway, and we went to California.

The days aboard the train were pretty good. The nights were dreadfully hot, with Bobby and me in the upper bunk behind velvet curtains, one head at each end.

I was sick almost the whole time in California, in bed at my Uncle Gene's house and not even comforted by the yellow Chinese rag doll he brought me. And there in bed, whenever I heard the sound of a train, I was sure it was going to leave its tracks and come get me, and Daddy would have to assure me again.

2

A wonderfully jolly officer lived in the quarters above us in our quadruplex at Fort Benning. When I saw him in the mornings, he would squat right down to my eye level and say, "Who's going to be the goodest girl in school today?" That would put determination into the heart of any red-blooded American kindergartener.

And he had a *Victrola*, which we didn't have but didn't need, because through the thin walls we could hear his perfectly well. So he loved to play our favorite records and then ask us later if we liked them: songs like—

> Got no boat, I can't float,
> What do I care?
> My sweetie turned—me—down. . . .

or,

> I found a million-dollar baby
> In the five and ten cent store. . . .

Whenever we had company, if we were out-of-doors I would tease, "Daddy, I want to do my trick. Daddy, I want to do my trick." I gave him no peace until he let me "show off"—by swinging by my knees from his bent right arm.

In termite country like Georgia, the quarters were built on posts with crawl space underneath, where the Barker children and I crawled in and played doctor once.

Once. Mother caught us.

I was in bed a long time with a combination of measles, strep throat, and bronchitis. I remember how hot I felt, and how my fingers trembled when I tried to hold my dolls. The doctor would occasionally come to the door and say, "You feelin' better today, Sugar?" and then amble away.

Finally my parents changed doctors, and the new one bent over me, and gave me medicines, and eventually I got well.

For a long time Mother and Daddy had promised me I could have a little red bathing suit when I got to fifty pounds. It seemed to take forever! I just couldn't eat that much. When I finally got to fifty pounds, we were just ready to leave for Annapolis, where we spent our summers. It was exciting to get my little red bathing suit and pack it for Annapolis.

Early on when we got to Annapolis the first time, Mother sent me to the store on the corner for something. When I came out I started for home in the opposite direction—and walked, until I came to the gate of the U.S. Naval Academy.

Where did I live? I didn't know.

Who were my parents? I knew *that.*

How to find them, that was the question. They sat me on a desk and fed me an ice-cream cone, until my daddy arrived.

I could hardly wait until I got to try out my little red bathing suit. Mother took Bobby and me to a beach at the Chesapeake Bay. From the car we hopped in our bare feet through the mud and grass and into the water—a swimming area fenced off with chicken wire (or something) to keep swimmers in and the jellyfish out. I couldn't swim, but I could float on my back with my eyes shut. Soon I had unknowingly floated out over my head, out over the fencing.

Mother at that moment became the lifeguard of the day (there was no other), determined to save me the only style she knew. She swam out to me, grabbed my little red bathing suit at the tummy, and windmilled it back to shore, with me going *up,* under, *up,* under.

I still think of that as a traumatic experience, but I was wet cement—and *Mother saved me.*

Sometimes Bobby and I would walk to an Annapolis pier with a bucket and string and catch crabs. The bad part was later, when Mother would put them into a big kettle of boiling water and pop the lid on—and I could still hear them scrabbling on the kettle sides!

Bobby and I would roller-skate for hours those long summer days, and Saint George's campus, where Daddy was writing books in an office, was the best place to skate. But the big trees buckled up the sidewalks, and I would trip and fall so often that my Mother finally sewed me some brown knee pads, so my scabs would begin to heal up.

Colonel Bond, who had hired Daddy to write, loved to come to our house and make us suppers of crab cakes and iced tea. They had to go together, because the crab cakes were so spicy-hot, you had to have a swallow of iced tea with every bite to put out the fire.

But it was a secret thrill: otherwise in the childhood of the Sweet children, none of us were ever allowed to have iced tea until we could gallop on a horse.

3

I was a dreamy child. (That sounds more positive than saying "half with it.") When the Fort Benning School recess time would come I would often go sit on the post bus, waiting to go home. After school I would think it was recess and go play on the playground, and then I'd have to go telephone and say, "Mother, I missed the bus again; I thought it was recess. . . ."

First grade was definitely marred for me. I had broken my arm, and I couldn't unbutton my bloomers. (You didn't call them panties yet.) I had to *go,* and I was in total misery, and Mother had said ask Mrs. Gridley to help me, but I just couldn't.

Eventually the inevitable happened, and Mrs. Gridley hung my bloomers to dry on the old stove, where all the children could see. I thought I'd die. Besides, when I got home Mother's supersharp nose sniffed the air and she asked, "Anne, did you . . . ?"

As the old proverb says, "Be sure your sins will find you out."

Second grade was a little better. Miss Stoner was younger and prettier and nicer. I remember once when roll was being taken, to which of course we each answered "here" when our name was called. Hazel Taylor and I were talking, which we weren't supposed to do. We completely gave it away, to our embarrassment, when Hazel's name was called in the middle

of her sentence about her new dress, and she called out "YEL-
LOW!"

Do playgrounds still have "giant strides," a maypole-type
thing that has handles at the ends of chains, and children swing
around the pole? Elizabeth Ann Bradley (General Omar's
daughter) was pushing me, and I was swinging higher and
higher—and then my hands got tired.

"Stop pushing! Let me down!" I cried, but somehow the message didn't get through. So I let go—and slid face first into
gravel, with the rim of my smashed glasses opening up a cut
over my right eye. Before long Miss Stoner had swooped me up
and was carrying me into the school building.

"You don't have to carry me; there's nothing wrong with my
legs," I remember saying.

Miss Stoner sounded absolutely terrified: "You might faint!
I'm afraid you're going to faint!"

I didn't; I didn't even know what it would be like; but for
years after when anything happened to me, I was deathly afraid
that the worst of all possible bad things might happen—I might
faint!

By the time Daddy was transferred to Fort Leavenworth,
Kansas, he and Mother had surrendered their lives to Jesus
Christ and had started in a new direction in their feelings and
goals. But I wasn't too aware of this yet, and at Fort Leavenworth third grade turned out to be my worst grade. Well, third
and fourth were my worst. The post school there was going
through a "progressive" phase, and Bobby was skipped over
seventh grade because he was so smart, while I was getting
*D*s and *F*s.

One of the subjects I was flunking was arithmetic, and Daddy
told me if I got an *A* he'd give me a wristwatch. I told Miss
Mayes, the teacher, and sure enough she gave me an *A*. Daddy
always proudly said that I was the one who put the "tick" in
"arithmetic."

But Miss Mayes was the kind of teacher who stood at the front of the room crying, while the boys jumped from desk top to desk top, throwing blackboard erasers at each other. I don't think I learned any arithmetic that year.

But the worst was that we changed classrooms for every subject, like college kids, and I would stand in the hallway between periods, jostled and confused and wringing my hands, trying to remember where to go next.

I made a pitiful attempt for a while to get status that year: I would eat ants. For anyone willing to watch, I would pop one in and hold my mouth open so they could see the thing squirming helplessly—probably from being pinched or maybe overwet. Then I'd swallow it.

This only drew a crowd for a short while.

Mother had discovered that year that I had taught myself to play "Silent Night" on the piano, melody in the right hand and chords in the left, so she hustled Bobby and me into piano classes. They really were classes (this, too, was progressive), and we all learned together to sight sing, play rhythm instruments, make music-history scrapbooks, and so on, before we had individual piano lessons. And we sat in fours at card tables which had keyboards painted on all four sides, and learned to read music and play whole pieces which we had never heard. When we finally graduated to pianos, we could play quite well what we were hearing for the first time!

In class, our teacher would also occasionally give us the treat of hearing her play pieces she had made up on the strings of her grand piano. ("Now the black magician chases her into the tower. . . . Now she screams. . . .")

Later we heard the teacher had gone crazy.

In our Fort Leavenworth quarters we lived upstairs, and I remember leaning over the iron railing of the porch, often dreaming of flying down on my own power.

Bobby rammed around with his best friend, Buddy Reed, but after school I loved to curl up with a book.

Sometimes my frequent fantasies would be cut short by baby sister Mary Alice's command, "Anne, 'top 'taring!"

I was by no means physically brave. Once I irritated a girl, and she began to beat up on me. I followed my first instinct to turn my back and put my hands over my head. But in my nervousness, I knocked my own glasses off, and they fell to the ground and broke. Later I went up to her front door and gave her mother a note, "telling" on her, and saying she had broken my . . . I couldn't spell it, so I drew a picture of glasses.

Another time some boys picked on me after school; and as I walked home, I was very close to crying. Bobby came racing up behind me and slapped my back to say "hi," and that did it: that broke the dam of tears. At first he was aghast, thinking he'd made me cry. But when I explained the problem, he chased the worst offender, sat on him, and beat him up.

Bobby was wonderful.

Daddy came home one day looking very grave. He held two telegrams in his hand and went straight past us to Mother. One said that her father had died (until then our only living grandparent).

The other said he'd been ordered to Hawaii. From then on my dreams were of lying under coconut trees, playing ukuleles.

4

We took a whole month to travel (Daddy had accumulated leave), and first we drove from Kansas to Washington, D.C., and saw Colonel Bond (the crab-cakes and iced-tea man, who had retired and moved there).

Mrs. Bond had put into her will that I was to receive her grand piano, but she lived so long, she outlived the piano, and I never got it.

Then we sailed on an Army transport ship from New York harbor. The Caribbean waters were rough and everybody was vomiting—even over the deck chairs. In Panama I saw my friend Hazel Taylor, who'd answered "yellow" to roll call; her daddy was now stationed in the Canal Zone.

Through the Canal Zone we went and on up to San Francisco to visit my very favorite Uncle Gene, who was like Daddy's twin: tall, laughing, gray-haired and gentle-voiced. Uncle Gene always liked me as much as Daddy did. (He is eighty-four now, and still calls me his "little Anne.")

And by the time we set sail from San Francisco for Hawaii, I had my own group of fans, who welcomed me back aboard like a famous person: I had found an old upright piano by the dining room, and all the ship stewards would gather around, keeping me playing their favorite songs during their off hours. When we

docked in Honolulu they gave me a celluloid Kewpie doll to
remember them by.

"How do you dance a hula?" was almost my first question of
the girl in whose parents' quarters we stayed while we house
hunted. Pretty soon I could do "King Kamehameha" and "Little Grass Shack" and a bunch more. Bobby picked up a ukulele,
and we taught each other, and he bought a lauhala hat, and we
considered ourselves natives.

Did you catch *house hunted?* Daddy didn't want quarters on
the post; he thought it would be fun to live in nearby Wahiawa
and be native, too. A really lovely home turned up, on grounds
owned by the California Packing Corporation, which canned
Del Monte pineapples. The president of C.P.C. lived on one
side of us and the vice-president on the other, and they each
had girls my age, Marian and Dorothy.

The three houses were approached by a long, winding road,
lined with stately royal palms, and the spacious grounds were
kept meticulously by Mr. Tagashi, whose house was in the back.

He brought fresh bananas to our back door every morning!

Bare feet! Sunshine! Hours in the sandpile, skipping rope,
playing jacks, and having our "club" in the "purple tree," a
huge jacaranda which never seemed to quit blooming. Marian
and Dorothy forced me out of my dreams and into the Hawaiian
climate. C.P.C. only rented that house to Army officers who had
daughters the age of Marian and Dorothy; I made us qualify, so
there I *was.*

They were good for me. I soon learned the terrific intrigues
of being three fifth-grade girls: secrets, club memberships, twos
against ones, with the groupings constantly shifting. In that
jungle you got political to survive! It was a brand-new world.

Occasionally boys ventured into the grounds, and from them
we learned bad words, and things that people did in secret in
the dark of night—even kids.

But not *me!* There was *Mother* to contend with. Still, to make sure, Bobby and I kept between us a wood carving of three little monkeys depicting SPEAK NO EVIL, SEE NO EVIL, HEAR NO EVIL. The information from all the Bible classes Mother taught hadn't gotten to us much yet, but *Mother had.*

What a lady Mother was! Daily, all her life, she did her dark hair beautifully and dressed in girdle and hose, only varying cotton housedresses with dressier ones. She rose very early for Bible study; she presided over the house and did shopping in the mornings and early afternoons. By mid-afternoon she bathed, put on a nicer dress, and sat in the living room, embroidering or crocheting or reading. She was in her chair by the time we got home from school, so she was forever available. We didn't need her much, but *she was there.* And her presence was a constant reminder that if we were bad, *we'd get it.*

Vaguely we kids heard of dust storms and depression in the "States." It meant nothing to us, but I remember feeling sorry for anyone who wasn't in the Army. (Being in the Army and sheltered from dust storms in Hawaii were somehow connected in my mind.) I would look at other children and wonder if they knew where their next meal was coming from. I worried that Marian and Dorothy, the first two civilian children I had really known, must have secret insecurities because their daddies were just "misters."

I have two conflicting memories of my performance those years.

One concerns Mother, who spanked me and scolded me often. (I needed it all. My room was always a hopeless mess, and I forgot things a lot.) Occasionally, the rumblings rose to storm level, and once Mother said, "Anne, I absolutely cannot understand you!" and went out into the bougainvillea arbor to cry.

The other memory is when our Plymouth's mileage gauge had gotten to 6,006 miles, and Daddy commented, "Look, Anne, the numbers are symmetrical."

"No, they're not, Daddy," I said. "To be symmetrical, one of the sixes would have to be backward."

Daddy was dumbfounded. He raved about my artistic eye, how sensitive my visual perception was, and said I would probably grow up to be something famous, and he even told his friends about it in front of me.

It made my tummy feel strangely warm and delicious.

5

Mother drove fifty miles nightly for two weeks over tortuous island roads to hear Dr. Donald Grey Barnhouse, a famous preacher visiting Honolulu. Always she took Bobby or me along. One night, twisting through Kipapa Gulch in a driving tropical rain, she told me that we would eventually be joined by a new little brother or sister. One sentence, no embellishments.

I didn't reply, but I thought a lot about it, and through the coming months I watched and wondered and created daydreams about what had happened. . . .

Bobby and I started piano lessons from a Mr. Resta, a warrant officer, who drove all the way from Fort Shasta, near Honolulu, to teach the two of us.

My first lesson I careened proudly through a bunch of numbers, including my favorite (which was really impressive) "Tea Time Waltz." Gently he explained to Mother that my training had been very poor (*what?* all those jazzy class lessons, and especially the card table thing?); and to my humiliation, he started me way back with simple songs, putting a rubber ball inside my palm, and making me raise my fingers like hammers.

Even when Hallowe'en came on music-lesson night, there was no reprieve. *(Round the hand, knuckles high; the fingers must fall like hammers.)* Bobby and I learned so many scales that it took us half an hour a day just to play them through.

During our lessons Mr. Resta would wander into another room, calling back that we had used the wrong finger, or played a B flat instead of a B. Eventually he corralled five-year-old Mary Alice and had her playing beautifully in a few months.

One night Mr. Resta brought me a book of Robert Louis Stevenson's children's poems, and also a blank music book. He asked me to set a certain poem to music. After he left I didn't want to go to bed but get right at it! From then on I tossed off weekly compositions for him, but before long he brought me up short.

"Anne," he said, "I can't accept that. 'How do you like to go up in a swing?' This sounds like a Sousa march. Make the swing go back and forth."

So I was less than perfect! I settled down then. There was something more to this thing than putting notes on paper. I labored. I thought.

Thousands of compositions later, I think "The Swing" is still one of my better ones.

6

Grammar school at Leilehua School was small-time. Mrs. Havlichek kept soap and a coffee can of water on the open windowsill and washed her hands out the window—that's how casual it was.

But moving into seventh grade, I was asked right off to be the accompanist for the high-school glee club. That was big-time! I practiced for hours on the first song assigned me, "Come to the Fair." The left hand really leaped around. I got it down cold and was playing it brilliantly with the glee club, when the director stopped us all.

"Anne, you're almost a full measure ahead of the rest of us," he said.

You mean I had to do all that leaping around and watch him, too? I had had no idea it would be so involved. That year was one of my Life Challenges.

Mother said, "Anne, I'm going to the hospital to have the baby, and I've made a tomato casserole for supper. It's in the oven, and at five o'clock turn the oven on. At quarter of six it will be ready to eat."

Responsibility! I stewed around so much with details that it was six o'clock before I proudly put the casserole on the table, accompanied by Daddy's outrageous praise. But when he put the serving spoon into it, it was stone-cold. I'd forgotten to turn the oven on!

The next afternoon Daddy came home with the news that we had a new baby sister, Margaret Burton. (Burton was his middle name.) I raced for the door to spread the news and was stopped by the need for political strategy. Whom did I tell first? I remember the moment of agonizing at the front door, before I turned left to tell Marian. Then together we raced right to tell Dorothy.

Dorothy was mad at me for quite a while.

What do we call the new baby? *Margaret* seemed too formal. Bobby named her: *Margie* pronounced like *Marjie.* He told his high-school teachers the next day, "Well, I'm the eldest of four this morning."

Bobby had gained a lot of stature by now. He had Daddy's gentle, winsome dignity and Mother's gorgeous good looks, and people said he was the sweetest, handsomest fifteen-year-old they'd ever seen. He looked fabulous in his white Sunday suit with his tan skin and thick black hair.

That year Bobby made Eagle Scout, was president of his junior class, won a lot of ribbons jumping in horse shows, and had his first girl friend, Florence Bigelow. She could have been his sister, with her dark good looks and gentle laugh. They rode their horses a lot together, and when we left Hawaii, she gave him a Kodak picture of herself.

On the way home, sailing as we had come through the Panama Canal and up to New York, I had a full month to fall in love, twelve-year-old style.

He was a cute brunette soldier who often sunned himself on the front deck, along with dozens of others. Leaning over the rail of the superstructure, I unabashedly watched him and daydreamed about him. He was too far away for communication—heavens! I would have died first before speaking to him, anyway. But I heard another soldier shout his name once: "Caroline."

Caroline. Suddenly it was a wonderful, he-man nickname for a guy. I wondered if he was from North or South Carolina, and if he spoke with a southern accent.

For a long time I dreamed that he had fallen for me, too. In spite of our age difference, he had searched for me, found me, and respectfully told my father he would wait any length of time, until I was old enough for him to claim me.

Delicious!

The Washington assignment was a thrill to Daddy; it meant that after being a student at the War College for a school year, he would probably eventually be a general. We lived in a little house on a hill (ugh! Washington rental costs!), and I went to junior-high school with *all* civilians.

My Latin teacher was tremendous! We said the Lord's Prayer every day in unison:

"Pater noster, Qui es in coelis, sanctificatur nomen Tuum. . . ."

And when there was leftover time, we sang the current hit songs in Latin: *"Quis in via venit?"* ("Who's that comin' down the street?") with its jazzy chorus,

Da-di-a, pater agitat;
Da-di-a, mater agitat;
Da-di-a, tu agitas,
Da-di-a, ego agito!

Pop swings it, mom swings it, you swing it, I swing it! *Wow!* School could be hip!

Then I fell in love at a little closer range with David Thompson, who sat in the first row in the glee club. I was quite a few rows behind him. Oh, the back of his head . . . !

One of my moments rose to a dizzying height and stopped still, when we were singing, "There's a long, long night of waiting until my dreams all come true, 'Til the day when I'll be going down that long, long trail with you"—and David turned around and looked straight at me—a long, straight look.

A long look . . . with his solemn blue eyes on mine.
The moment was as long as a quiet summer afternoon. . . .
I couldn't breathe.
My whole body tingled and buzzed in the stillness.
I felt proposed to. . . .
That carried me through a whole year of daydreams

7

I was chosen to be the Pink Lady in an operetta the glee club put on, with a solo to sing! I had long hair to my waist, and I wore a cheesecloth gown which Mother made me, and I arrived on stage in a spectacular swan-shaped boat, which I pushed along with my feet to propel.

But I got a horrendous cold at the last moment, probably from nervousness; and after I croaked and wheezed through my solo, as the applause died away, somebody in the audience said, "Huh! I sure wouldn't clap for *her!*"

What really saved that year for me, though, was Barbara Howard. Our family had arrived at the Fourth Presbyterian Church the first Sunday we were in Washington. Barbara bounced up to Bobby and me to invite us to Christian Endeavor —"C.E." (Once Bobby and I were with Barbara in choir, we learned that that was part from the choir loft you picked the new ones out of the congregation each week and bounced down after the service and invited them to whatever. We did it all year.)

But especially Barbara could bounce,—irrepressible Barbara, a high schooler with Irish-red hair.

Quickly Bobby and I joined her in going by bus and streetcar on Sunday nights to C.E., on Wednesday nights to prayer meeting, on Thursday nights to choir practice, and on Saturdays to roller-skate and sightsee with all the C.E. kids in downtown Washington. Barbara loosened up Bobby's gentle dignity, and she made me forget my inhibitions. We both needed Barbara!

After meetings we'd go too far on the bus by mistake—for adventures. Once we sashayed into a train engine in the Washington station, and got the engineer to show us how it worked.

We saw some children playing hopscotch and jumped off the bus to join them.

We explored the caverns of a backstage, when a door was left open.

Often on a bus or streetcar we sang trios—and then passed the hat all around to the passengers.

Once Barbara brought three old scarves, two for her head and mine, and one for Bobby's neck, and made us talk "foreign" for the public's benefit.

Sometimes she limped—to attract attention.

Barbara talked to anybody, and that year Bobby and I caught something of her bubble. We were truthfully always a little more fun after knowing Barbara.

We were still wet cement!

Barbara loved the Lord—and quickly Barbara loved Bobby, too. The first love was lifelong, but the second was not to be; Bobby was still carrying Florence Bigelow's Kodak picture.

That year Bobby played the big pipe organ for all his high-school assemblies, and graduated at sixteen with all *A*s. Then we moved to Fort Sam Houston, Texas.

How long is childhood? Have I recounted enough? Letting the memories flow out has told me a lot about myself.

I realize, for instance, that I've never been without a peer male model. When I was born, Bobby was three; I always had him. When he was killed in World War II at twenty-four, I was just becoming engaged to Ray. For a while after marriage, my brother was still more in my heart than my husband—I'd adored him so much, and we'd been so close. But gradually Ray won me, down deep inside, by his true godliness and his unswerving love for me.

Now today as I write, it's Ray's fifty-seventh birthday, and would have been Bob's sixtieth; the two men of my life were both born on July 9. They are—were—both stronger than me; I have leaned and learned and been propelled along by their companionship and their drives.

My childhood "cement prints" are right there inside me still.

Sometimes I am the glowing, acknowledging pianist aboard ship, being presented with a Kewpie doll.

Sometimes I'm the little third-grader between classes, wringing her hands uncertainly among people all rushing to their certain places.

Sometimes Mother, now in heaven, keeps me from a questionable act; or Daddy, there, too, gives me the hope of excellence.

I am the hider under the house, doing furtive things, and getting caught—by the Lord.

I am the cocky plunger ahead, to discover I'm a measure ahead of the choir. (Recently I didn't check with Ray and signed two book contracts at once, both due *first.*)

I am the politic, weighing my words; the dreamer reprimanded by a two-year-old; the basic onlooker being forced out of my shell into participation—and feeling exhilarated.

I am the girl who gets her status from her wonderful big brother-husband.

I am also the girl with recognizable creativity inside, prodded to produce by the Mr. Restas of this world—music agents and book publishers.

Inside I am still little Betty Ann. Yes, I see my cement prints . . . and I remember how I got them.

A Project for You

Before you go any further in your reading, it might be really helpful to you to think about your own early days when you were wet cement.

1. Pull out a tablet of paper. Go off by yourself for a while. Shut your eyes and—back in your mind—reach for your earliest memories.

2. Put them down, both good and bad. On a few pieces of paper, you can begin to see how your life has been, and what has helped make you what you are.

You'll understand yourself better, but at this point, don't be discouraged. Maybe the wonderful "God of hope" wants you to read the rest of this book!

Section II

About You . . .

8

You think about your childhood, and maybe a child darts across your path, or across your mind.

Maybe this child is your own offspring, or your own by adoption.

Maybe he's unborn as yet, inside of you or your wife.

Maybe he's your own child fully grown, on his own now.

Maybe you're not a parent—but he's the child of your brother, or sister, or friend.

Maybe he's your grandchild.

Maybe you're a teacher, and he's your student.

This book is not a "child-raising book" for parents only. It's to give you help in handling the children in your life; so when I say "your child," you can translate it *nephew* or *student* or *little friend* or whatever.

I want to give you a technique of helps so powerful that you'll have to use it with great care. Otherwise it will backfire on you, as it's been known to do.

That child of yours is helpless in the hands of the people around him. He is pliable to their shaping; they set his mold. What will he become?

That's what Abraham Lincoln asked—who never paid more than minimum courtesy to the adults whom he passed on the street, but when he passed a child, he stepped out of the way and doffed his hat.

"These adults I know," he said, "but who knows what the children may become?"

These little ones, kicking in their cribs or racing around—they are tomorrow's world, our most precious possession, most powerful potential.

Oh, the specialness of children! I know a couple who, in the darkest days of threatened business failure, had a new baby boy, Chris. Chris was their comic relief! They said then, and they've been repeating it ever since, Chris was God's gift in those days to preserve their sanity.

Who says anything as great as kids say it?

Our Sherry once sat in her breakfast chair, picking all the raisins out of her Cream of Wheat (she didn't like raisins), and arranging them in a gooey little line around the edge of her cereal bowl.

"There," she said, "look at 'em all, standing on the Word of God."

And how can we help but be tender with these funny little people, when they try so hard, and get things so mixed up?

I stopped by one of our Sunday-school classes a while back, just when kids were dismissed.

"What did you learn today?" I asked one little guy. "Can you say a Bible verse?"

He was willing—but he sure was confused. He said, "Be ye kind—one, two, buckle my shoe."

But the awesome thing is that they receive their impressions of life from us—even their impressions of what makes godliness. One little girl said, "My mother is very religious. She goes to play Bingo at church every week, even if she has a cold!" (From *Dear Pastor,* selected by Bill Adler.)

It's scary! They get all their impressions of life from the big people around them.

Nobody asks questions like children. One asked, "Who does God pray to? Is there a God for God?" (Another from *Dear Pastor.*)

By the time our Buddy was five, I'd finally put a lot of his questions into a song:

Mommy, what's a claptrap?
Mommy, where's north? . . . What's RO-mance?
Mamma, did you ever see a native?
Mommy, what do ducks do?
Mommy, what's spring? . . . What's grease?
Mamma, were you ever buried alive?
Mamma, am I a space cadet? . . . What's space?
Mommy, when will I grow up?
Mommy, how many pushups can you do?
Mamma, do you know the President? Why not?
Where are the vitamins in my cereal?
Mommy, if a crab's leg falls off, does it grow back? . . .
    Mommy, what's a crab?
If I go to the moon, will I pop?
Mamma, did you ever hit a snake? . . . Why not?

Copyright Anne Ortlund 1954. All rights reserved.

Used by permission.

And how they charm us! No one talks like a child. They speak Childese, the most intriguing and complicated language in the world—a language which dies with every generation and is resurrected with every new one. Who but a child could write, "I hope to go to heaven some day, but later than sooner"? (from *Dear Pastor*).

Well, they are God's wonderful gift to us. Certainly they make us what we would never be, if they weren't watching us and copying us!

They are the arrows from our bows, with their direction dependent on our guidance.

They are the receivers of our batons, when we begin to tire.

They are tomorrow's heroes and rescuers and achievers—or else tomorrow's thieves and saboteurs and loafers.

9

You found, as you thought about your childhood, a lot of mistakes and problems. How can you guide your child to a life better than yours?

Let's change the figure of speech for a moment. Instead of wet cement,—

He's the rocket on a launching pad, ready to take off. How high will he go? If you have six children, each will soar to a different level; the genes and personal experiences and so many ingredients in the mix will give each one a different potential.

God planned it that way! He says, "For we are God's workmanship, created in Christ Jesus to do good works, which God prepared in advance for us to do" (Ephesians 2:10).

How can you free your child, to launch him into his full potential? How can you counteract the downward drag of bad influences you don't even know about—or, if this is a little friend of yours—possibly the bad influence of his own poor parents? What can you do, to release him to soar?

The way he thinks about himself later on, before God, will have been very much influenced by the way you've talked to him, treated him, handled him. When he's young, unconsciously you size him up, and then, unconsciously, you impose your limitations on him.

"Freddie," you may say wearily, "at this rate you'll never get past junior-high school." That impression goes into the wet cement of his mind. If he catches the idea from you often, he may really believe it—and never get past junior-high school.

"Charlie," you may say, "just the way you talk sometimes, I can hear in you the makings of a great man. I'll bet you'll influence a lot of people for good—for God, too." He'll catch that from you and believe it—and it may well come true

Your child is wet cement!

When your Freddie or Charlie or Sue came into the world, he or she was pure potential. He had few limits. But after a brief period of admiring and cuddling, all too soon life settled down.

He bugged you by crying too much. He spit up, and he dirtied his pants, and he pulled things out of drawers; and before long it was easy to convey to him that he's an irritation, an inconvenience—a drag!

Then think about the things that begin coming out of your mouth.

"Boy," you may say to others, "if I had two more like him, I'd be a screaming meemie!"

"How come he can spit up so much? I didn't put that much into him. He's gotta be manufacturing his own!"

"This kid knows every drawer in this house. Nothing is safe any more. For every one thing I tie down, she's figured out six new disasters!"

"I'd like to go with you, Virginia, but it's just too hard to drag Barry around, and I can't afford a sitter."

By the tone of voice, then by the words, he catches the implications sooner than you expect. And earlier than you dream, he begins to get degrading impressions of himself:

"I'm a bother to the people around me."

"I'm bad."

"I can't do things the bigger kids do; I'm inferior."

"They don't like my habits; they don't like *me.*"

"I get punished if I experiment. I'm afraid. I'm shy."

These aren't things he could verbalize yet, but they're impressions in the wet cement.

Think about it: whether your child is tiny or college-age or anywhere in between, *verbal put-downs are a subtle but very real form of child abuse.*

Last Sunday's sermon (not one of Ray's) included a story about an eagle egg lost from its nest and put into the nest of a prairie chicken. So the egg was hatched with the rest, and the little eagle grew up thinking he was a prairie chicken, too. He scratched in the dirt with the rest for seeds and worms, and he flew in just brief stretches by a great deal of thrashing with his wings.

One day when the eagle was grown, he saw a great eagle soaring in the sky.

"What's that?" he asked in wonder, watching the eagle catch the air currents, almost without effort.

"Oh, that's an eagle," was the answer. "You and I can never be like that."

And so he never was. And he lived his life and died, thinking he was a prairie chicken.

Also last week, we had dinner with some friends we hadn't seen for a while. In fact, we had never seen their beautiful little three-year-old Donna.

"Donna will come to you, Anne," said her mother, "but not o Ray. For some reason she just doesn't like men."

Sure enough, Donna ran straight into my arms, and she'd have nothing to do with Ray. Why not? She was being programmed. I pray that it may not make a problem when Donna is sixteen—or thirty-six.

Because now Donna is wet cement.

How does a child get turned off from reading and books? Maybe through the six years previous to first grade, books were associated with put-downs and punishment:

"Scott! Bad boy! You colored in this book!"

"Carrie! Stop tearing that lovely page!"

The lesson learned: "Books are associated with hurts. I don't like books."

Some of the no-no's produce healthy fears: don't run into the street; don't touch a stove. But what are the things we're saying —or neglecting to say—that may simply hinder? Your child, too, is wet cement!

10

Let's have a little study in the life of David, the psalmist of the Bible, to see what childhood impressions can do.

David was a man of emotional ups and downs. He had moods of high exultation and of terrible depression. His psalms reveal them both. Now "in all things God works for the good of those who love him . . ." Romans 8:28, and when God had David write down all those psalms, the variety of them has ever since helped believers through every possible emotion.

But why would a godly fellow like David suffer so much inward pain?

Look at his background. Number One, his father Jesse was probably a loser. What makes me think so? Well, his great-grandfather Boaz had been a very wealthy man. (See his story in the Book of Ruth.) Yet David's father Jesse was so poor that instead of using a hired man, he made his own son David tend his "few sheep" (1 Samuel 17:28). Where did the money go in two short generations? Maybe Jesse didn't hang on to it too well.

Besides, whenever King Saul and others wanted to degrade David they called him that "son of Jesse" (1 Samuel 22:7, 8, 9; 25:10). David's father must not have been much of a man.

And have you noticed the place David had within this family of little distinction? Picture it:

The great prophet Samuel sends word, "Tell Jesse of Bethlehem that I'm coming to his town" (1 Samuel 16:1-4).

Everybody in town hears the news, and they wonder what they've done wrong!

By the time Samuel arrives, not no-account Jesse but all the important men of the town are knocking over each other to be first in line, and they ask him, "D-d-do you come in peace?"

"Yes," says Samuel. "I've come to offer a sacrifice, and it's Jesse and his sons whom I want to consecrate themselves and come to the sacrifice with me."

Of all people, the fellows think, *why would he pick somebody like Jesse?*

Jesse and his sons scramble around to consecrate themselves and show up at a sacrifice with *the* prophet Samuel.

And yet in this biggest event in their lives, the father and brothers didn't bother to include David. He didn't matter; he could just stay out and look after the sheep, as usual.

But God is whispering in the prophet's ear, "No, Samuel, none of these boys is the future king of Israel."

"Don't you have any more sons?" Samuel asks.

"Well, there's one more," says Jesse—and some translations say Jesse calls him "the youngest," but the Hebrew word could just as well be translated "the least." Maybe David was third in line of the eight, or fifth, or sixth; we don't know. All we know is that he was considered the one who didn't matter, who didn't have to be included with the family. It's a real Cinderella story, isn't it!

Can you think what this would do to young David's ego? Do you think he might have been sitting out guarding those "few sheep" while crying bitterly, because he was left out of celebrating with the greatest prophet of his day? That young boy was wet cement.

No wonder when he was a grown man he wrote,

> O LORD, how many are my foes!
> How many rise up against me!

Psalms 3:1

Be merciful to me, LORD, for I am faint;
O LORD, heal me, for my bones are in agony.
My soul is in anguish.
How long, O LORD, how long?

6:2, 3

I am worn out from groaning;
all night long I flood my bed with weeping
and drench my couch with tears.

6:6

Help, LORD, for the godly are no more;
the faithful have vanished from among men.
Everyone lies to his neighbor;
their flattering lips speak with deception.

12:1, 2

And even the words that Jesus quoted on the cross:

"My God, my God, why have you forsaken me?"

22:1

David struggled all his life with the hurts in his heart—and
no wonder, if we can gather anything from his childhood. He
must have had plenty of damaging cement prints inside.

How can you keep from injuring your child?

How can you put in impressions that will build into him great
expectations for his adult life?

11

Inside of your child is a subconscious mind. It's a *storage box* into which people and events are constantly putting ideas.

I heard a cute story the other day about how we "program" the minds of children. The pastor was at the front of the church giving a children's sermon.

"Now, children," he said, "what has a bushy tail, and likes to climb in trees, and hides nuts?"

There was a total silence.

The pastor tried again: "You know, children: he's sometimes gray, with little ears, and he runs in trees swishing his big, bushy tail?"

The kids just looked around at each other helplessly, and the adults began to titter.

Finally a little girl raised her hand. "Pastor," she said, "I know we're supposed to say 'Jesus,' but it sure sounds like a squirrel to me."

Yes, we adults are constantly impressing children's minds with our ideas! But that's not really the point of what I want to say about input into the subconscious.

Once I was holding our baby Sherry too close to the stove, and a burner was on. Before I realized what was happening, she had put her little hand down on that electric burner. Did she scream! Fortunately, the doctor was right across the street, and he was treating that hand in record time.

But something more than heat was being impressed into Sherry. Into the storage box of her subconscious mind went the information: "Stove burners are not to be touched. They can hurt."

The next time she was tempted to touch a burner, her subconscious would marvelously select that information out of the box, feed it to her computer brain, and by reflex action her hand would draw back.

So what goes into the subconscious mind soon becomes the habits which govern human behavior. God's Word spells this out for us in many places. (Some of these may be found in Mark 7:21; Matthew 15:19; Psalms 36:1–3.) He tells us that out of the subconscious within us come the actions which form habits and life patterns.

And every day your child is receiving new input to store away inside of him.

I was getting input placed into my storage box–
· When Daddy pulled the pup tent down on top of me;
· When that girl told me the Red Hands were after me;
· When the iced-tea ban was silently lifted as Daddy's authority gave way to Colonel Bond's;
· When Mother spanked me and scolded me—but sewed me a green dress and brown knee pads, and grabbed me by my little red bathing suit out of the Chesapeake Bay;
· When Bobby and I made a pact over the "speak-no-evil-see-no-evil-hear-no-evil" monkeys;
· When Mr. Resta demoted me to easy piano pieces and put a rubber ball inside my hand;
· When I discovered that people on streetcars laughed when Barbara and Bobby and I sang trios to them. . . .

So the input going into your child's storage box day by day, moment by moment, is forming the patterns by which he'll live his future life.

How impressionable children are! They are really helpless in the hands of those around them. They're so easily convinced, so pliable; they believe whatever they're told.

And how they absorb whatever goes into them! Have you watched *them* watch? Their mouths may hang open; they're not, like adults, aware of themselves—they're only aware of what they're watching—what's being fed into their computer.

And your child is in process, as a person. Every eight days he gets a new layer of skin. Every eight years every cell in his body has become new. Look at that child right now: since this time yesterday he has three million new blood cells.

He's growing; he's changing. He's wet cement! Set the habit patterns of his life. You can't *make* your child—God does; but you can feed him input.

If you don't, his friends will, and the television will, and movies will. . . .

And he'll either be improving constantly by the godliness and truth of your fresh input, or he'll keep repeating over and over what he was before, and deepening bad habits or going to worse ones.

Oh, little one! How precious you are, how important!

You are tomorrow's world.

You are the hope of your generation members who don't know the Lord. You are the potential to be salt, to be light, to speak up, to live out, to lift, to correct, to encourage, to change.

How should I treat you, to help you become this?

What should I say?

12

How? That's the important question. What is the new input that should go into his subconscious storage box? And how do you get it there?

The directing of a human is so crucial, it encompasses two directions: God-ward and child-ward.

First you pray. And continually you pray. Become a praying mother, a praying friend, a praying grandparent, or a praying surrogate parent! Pray as he's a newborn. Pray as he crawls and walks and runs off to school. Pray as he studies and makes friends and sets his own life course.

And it happens just about that fast! I wish I could remember a poem I read years ago in an old magazine. The gist of it was this:

> My newborn babe
> Struggles from my arms
> And toddles off to school.
> A tall young man accompanies her home.
> Their child brings me
> My glasses and shawl.

The first three lines of the poem cover about six years. The last three cover at least forty or fifty. So it is with child raising: the pace seems to accelerate!

Whatever stage he's in, let prayer cover it from now on. Whether your child is yet unborn or has long been an adult, cry to God for him!

My heart just melts when I think about Laura. I was speaking last year at a conference in Nebraska and mentioned something about Nels. Nels was fourteen at the time and already an awkward six feet tall. I don't know—we were just going through the usual agonies of child raising.

At the end of the meeting, up came this pretty young mother. "I'd like to pray for Nels," she said, "every day for the next year."

That's 365 prayers, and she had never seen me before and didn't know Nels at all!

She slipped a piece of her pink stationery into my hand. It said,

> Dear Anne,
> On this first day of the rest of Nels' life I will pray for him and you and Ray daily for one year (at least), April 17 to April 17, concerning your discipling him and about his personal growth, that he would be conformed to the image of Christ. In His love—

And she gave her name and address.

I pasted her letter in the GOALS section of my notebook, and occasionally through the year I sent her progress reports, and she sent me beautiful letters, spelling out the things God had led her to pray for Nels.

On the next April 17 I wired her flowers, and they crossed with her letter to me, saying that she wanted to pray for Nels daily for a second year!

I can't tell you how touched and moved I was/am. Any parent knows these are the tough years of insecurity and transition, and especially because our dear Nels went to Stony Brook School in New York last fall for tenth grade. He really needs to be shored up, and so do we.

I've kept Laura's most recent letter with me, since it arrived

two weeks ago. I want to quote part of it for you, to give you
a little of the flavor of what it might be for you to take on a
project of prayer for someone else's child. (Laura also has her
own children.)

She writes,

> I've got to tell you about one day a few weeks ago. I began
> to pray for Nels and waited for the Lord to show me what He
> wanted requested. Oftentimes they just flow out of Scripture
> I've been reading.
>
> But no requests came, just thanksgiving! The Lord
> prompted: Thank You for Nels. Thank You for creating him, for
> giving him life, for the way You formed him, for how Your hand
> has been upon him, for the personality You have given him, for
> the future You have for him and the ways You have for him to
> glorify You.
>
> That whole day the Lord just gave things to praise Him
> for concerning Nels. A couple of times I tried to sneak in a
> few requests, and it was as if God put His finger on my
> mouth (as if to say sh-h-h) and then gave more praise and
> thanksgiving!
>
> Now for some requests. (What joy!)
>
> That: Nels would listen and be careful to do the commands
> of the Lord (Deuteronomy 6:3).
>
> That: God give creative wisdom to you and Ray as parents.
>
> That: you would all relish the fun of being a family.
>
> That: Nels bring glory to You, Lord.
>
> That: his friends be godly and in their friendships have their
> interpersonal needs met. Nels' friends themselves (this was
> stimulated by your mentioning of Eric and promoted prayer for
> him).
>
> That: Nels be a delight to his parents (Proverbs) and open his
> mouth with wisdom (as the mouth reflects the heart).
>
> That: his heart be pure before the Lord.
>
> That: God give him an ever-increasing desire to serve the
> Lord with his whole heart, increasing through the years. . . .

That: God give him continued protection from evil and the evil one.

May God bless that boy! And may He bless you and Ray, also! . . .

There's a nice postscript to this story. Laura lives two thousand miles from our California home. A while back Ray and I were going to speak at a weekend conference in Nebraska and took Nels along. Laura and her family heard we were speaking, and drove a long way to attend one of the sessions.

She had no idea Nels would be with us! And after the meeting, she and Nels sat together and talked and got acquainted for a long time. Isn't God kind! Aren't His rewards and bonuses amazing!

And having Nels undergirded with Laura's daily intercession is one of the most wonderful gifts anybody's ever given us.

I think of my own childhood—of swinging cats by their tails and being scared spitless by locomotives—how much must have been negated and overcome by the strong prayers of my parents! Do you want to raise courageous, healthy, godly achievers?

Tell God about it.

13

Tell God about your child—and second, *tell your child.*
How he needs your support and affirmation! When he's new in
this world, his security is a very tenuous thing. Every child
needs heaps and gobs of affirmation. They need words! One
little boy wrote his pastor a letter: "Dear Pastor, Please say in
your sermon that Peter Peterson has been a good boy all
week. I am Peter Peterson" (another from Bill Adler's collec-
tion).

The impressions words make, as they go into his ears and
down into his heart and his concept of himself, are absolutely
crucial.

"As a [person] thinks in his heart, so is he" (*see* Proverbs 23:7;
see also Mark 7:21; Matthew 15:19; Psalms 36:1–3).

> We are not what we think we are, but WHAT WE
> THINK—WE ARE! Our heart secrets are the mold for
> our character and the index of our worth.
>
> The Keswick Calendar

Over and over, put specific information into his storage box.
I hadn't even clearly defined this technique when our first
three were growing up, and yet I thank the Lord that He
helped me do it somewhat. Over and over Ray and I told each

child separately, "I can hardly wait 'til you grow up. You're going to stand out in a crowd! You're going to love the Lord; you're going to lead others in spiritual things; you're going to be a wonderful Christian adult. We'll be so proud of you."

And it's true; each one of them has become that. We're telling our fourth child these things now.

But what if your child is just born, brand-new in your arms? Even when he's only grasping tone of voice and touch, how he needs your loving input! Nobody is more needy than a new-born. He is absolutely helpless, and dependent on you for all his early shapings.

Pearl Buck once wrote,

> . . . Upon a child in need I now bestow
> The means of living;
> Thus, in such giving,
> Life flows into life. . . .

And your life will flow into his. Tell him very specific things, to impress into him what you want him to be:

1. "You're such a wonderful baby."
2. "You're getting happier and more relaxed all the time."
3. "You *like* living at our house, don't you!"
4. "We *love* having you here!"
5. "Isn't Daddy [Mother] wonderful . . . isn't Brother wonderful . . . isn't Sister wonderful . . . !"
6. "God loves you . . . Jesus loves you . . . Mother loves you . . . Daddy loves you . . . Brother loves you . . . Sister loves you. . . ."
7. "Bed is a happy place; you love to sleep. . . ."
8. "Waking up is fun; now you'll have a good time. . . ."
9. "I'm so proud of you. . . ."

And over and over, hold him in your arms, rock him back and forth, and say, "I can hardly wait to see the wonderful grown-up you're going to be; oh, I'll be so proud . . . !"

So he doesn't understand? Maybe he does! And if not, *you* are forming the habits of positive affirming which will certainly mold your treatment of him when he's six months, two years, five, sixteen. . . . You will think twice before those degrading comments slip out of your mouth to hurt and misshape him. You'll be becoming the kind of parent you need to be, for his sake.

Say those affirmations over his first morning meal. Say them as you tuck him into bed at night with prayer (yes, even a newborn). You will form the habit of saying them, and affirmations of him will become your habitual way of life as a parent.

He's wet cement, you know—

And so are you.

A Project for You

1. *Talk to God about your child.* How will you make your praying very specific?

   a. If you're the parent, you may write out your daily prayers for your child. (Oh, I can't tell you how powerfully God has used my prayer life since I began writing my prayers, and since I've known specifically how I've talked to Him and what I've asked Him for!)

   b. Or you may wait on Him for direction; write out a very carefully specific prayer for that child, and hold it before the Lord every day, word for word.

   c. If you're not the parent, you may choose to pray one of these ways, anyhow, or you may decide on Laura's way: to covenant to pray for the child for a certain period of time. If you think the parent would be sympathetic to this, let him or her know; ask for prayer requests; and report in from time to time on what you're praying.

2. *Talk to your child*—or if he's yet unborn, get ready to. Make a specific list of affirmations which will begin not only to shape him, but to shape your handling of him.

If your child is toddler to twelve, start reading the next section!

14

If a child lives with criticism, he learns to condemn.
If a child lives with hostility, he learns to fight.
If a child lives with ridicule, he learns to be shy.
If a child lives with shame, he learns to feel guilty.
If a child lives with tolerance, he learns to be patient.
If a child lives with encouragement, he learns to
      have confidence.
If a child lives with praise, he learns appreciation.
If a child lives with fairness, he learns justice.
If a child lives with security, he learns to have faith.
If a child lives with approval, he learns to like himself.
If a child lives with acceptance and friendship, he learns to find
      love in the world.

DOROTHY LAW NOLTE

What's done to children they will do to society.

DR. KARL MENNINGER

So your little one is growing and changing. So will your affirmations grow and change.

Is he into the toddler stage? Some of your list of affirmations will be almost the same as for the newborn:

1. "You're such a wonderful boy [girl]."
2. "You're getting happier and more relaxed all the time."
3. "You *like* living at our house, don't you!"
4. "We *love* having you here!"
5. "Isn't Daddy [Mother] wonderful . . . isn't Brother wonderful . . . isn't Sister wonderful . . . ?"
6. "God loves you . . . Jesus loves you . . . Daddy loves you . . . Mother loves you . . . Brother loves you . . . Sister loves you. . . ."
7. "I'm so proud of you!"

But some will drop off and you might be adding others:

8. "How well you walk! . . . How well you talk! . . . How nicely you play! . . ."
9. "You're going to love school. . . ."
10. "You're getting to be so much fun. . . ."
11. "What a smart boy [girl] you are! . . ."
12. "You like other children; you like grown-ups, too."
13. "You're learning to love Jesus more and more."

Don't make the affirmations too idealistic or unrealistic.

Don't have too many—just a very few at a time.

Don't put on time limits; that pressures him. Your child must develop at his own pace.

See if you can slip in each affirmation once or twice a day.

Sally Folger Dye, writing about affirmations in *To Put Down or Build Up,* gives a good word:

> Practice creative ways of affirming and uplifting [him]. This is essential. Attributing goodness by creatively visualizing [him] as achieving his goals, and acting as if he is *progressing ahead of his actual progress* [italics mine] is helpful in giving [him] freedom to grow.

Do you catch the technique? You affirm the child at a level *higher than he is actually doing:* this gives him the freedom to

grow joyously up to that level! In *K-T Notes* Michael E.
Kolivosky and Lawrence T. Taylor wrote,

> Love them for what you are sure they will become.
> Blessed is the child whose parents' judgment is based on
> what the child will some day be.

This is exactly what our heavenly Parent does for us, His
children. He accepts us as "righteous" before we actually are
righteous. Romans chapters 3 to 8 spell out that God accepts us,
not because of our own goodness, but because He "imputes"
goodness to us; He counts it as so;—but that some day we will
actually be totally what He now sees us to be!

No wonder we who understand this, live in "hope." We are
free to grow toward what He already considers that we are. And
we know, no matter what the present struggles, that eventually
we'll get there.

Praise the Lord!

Shouldn't we also, on the basis of salvation through Christ, be
this generous to the struggling, less-than-perfect children of the
next generation? If our heavenly Parent forgives our debts,
shouldn't we also forgive our children's debts?

15

Support—but don't push. Affirmations are not to make your child "do things" faster. They are to give him emotional underpinnings for his life.

Childhood is like a college course. Let your younger child be himself, taking a general course, as in the freshman and sophomore years, exposed to many fields. Don't encourage him to specialize too soon.

When a freshman goes off to college for the first time, everything is new. He not only is going to have to learn mathematics, but where the dining room is, how many chapel cuts he can have, where he's to do his laundry, whether it's "in" to try out for a student office, what to wear—*everything.*

When a baby comes into this world, everything is new to him, too. He has to learn how you know when food's coming, whether people are nice or not; what day is for and what night is for; how to turn over; and later how to pull, how to push, how to confront another kid, and on and on.

One of the problems of childhood today is that when there are so many general things to learn, children are asked to specialize too soon.

Eda J. LeShan describes in her book *The Conspiracy Against Childhood* the fantastic "advantages" of our children: music lessons, scouts, zoos, beaches, record players, sandboxes—every gadget, every "important experience" possible. Then she describes the increase in teenage suicides, childhood ulcers, migraine headaches, adolescent crime, and drugs.

What has gone wrong? She says we are hell-bent on eliminating childhood.

We seem more and more determined to get children who will "produce" and who will "conform." We really like children best when they stop being children and become like adults. . . .

> There is no area in which our discontent, our impatience with growth shows up more clearly than in our attitudes toward learning. . . . We are in such a rush to educate our children that department stores are now selling special pillowcases and towels for children that say PLEASE TEACH ME TO READ—and then provide imprinted letters, numbers, words and clocks for telling time. A book that suggested that we start reading readiness at ten months sold 75,000 copies in a short time. Another book that promised to *Give Your Child a Superior Mind* gave careful instructions which would help a child read 150 words a minute, add, subtract, multiply and divide, understand fractions and simple algebra, all before the age of five. All a parent had to do was "make lessons a rigid part of the child's daily schedule, starting at 30 months of age."

When you think of it, their heads will start swimming soon enough! I saw a cartoon recently of a little fellow asking his pastor, "How many apostles are there under the metric system?"

Under the hairdryer I was reading the thoughts of a pediatrician:

> QUESTION: "Are children really learning to read, write, spell, do arithmetic, etc., at younger ages now-days?"
> ANSWER: "Certainly. Most children can be taught these skills long before school age. But we've never had so many young children before with nervous disorders and psychological problems."

And Dr. LeShan says there's no evidence that toddlers who read early are better readers by the time they're in sixth grade. By then the others have caught up.

So what *should* a two- to five-year-old be learning?

He should learn to know what he likes and what he doesn't; how to build with blocks; to paste; to climb, to swing; to run; to hop; to skip. . . .

He should learn to imagine: to pretend he's a policeman, a bus driver, a daddy. . . .

He should begin to learn how to deal with fear and love and jealousy and hatred and wonder. . . .

He should learn how to take simple things apart; how to pour; how to pile; how to push. . . .

Look at children in a church nursery at play. We're apt to say, "They should be *doing* something, *exposed* to something. We should take advantage of this valuable time."

They *are* doing something; they're encountering life. Dr. LeShan also declared,

> When a child moves into group play, when he shares or takes turns, when he recognizes another's pain or frustration, when he acts out his own conflicts, anxieties, fears, and confusions . . . he is doing the plain, hard, uncompromising *work* of growing up. . . . [Isn't this enough for one who has been alive in the world for just —say, thirty months?]

16

That's the negative: what *not* to do. Don't push.

So what do we do: to encourage them to grow inwardly, to become resourceful and creative, to think, to meditate, to lay the foundation for growing up well?

Don't push—just affirm them. Give them the sense that all is well, that their rate of progress is acceptable to you, that you like them just the way they are.

That's how God loves you: "just as you are." And you're to "accept one another just as Christ accepted you" (Romans 15:7). Accept your child!

We love tiny babies; three-year-olds we call brats or monsters. When did the change come? When they began to reach out, to experiment, to get into trouble.

Guide them—but be delighted in them! Let them know that life is to be reached for and drunk of deeply.

Aggressiveness is to be encouraged; fear is to be dealt with and overcome. When they're adults, you'll want them to be aggressive after God, aggressively seeking people to love, aggressively acting as salt in their community, absolutely unafraid to shout no! when sin presents itself.

So when they're small, affirmations will help give them courage for life.

Enthusiastic: that's how you want them to grow up. The word comes from *en Theo,* or "in God." Support them with words of faith, hope, and love, and in that framework—"in God"—they'll be ready to tackle anything.

Fears and cautions are built in at an early age—but so is courage! Tomorrow's world will be different—if your child has been released to experiment, to risk, to lead others, to pursue righteousness, to be an affecter for good in society, to go courageously after God.

Psalms 18:29 says it:

> With your help I can advance against a troop;
>> with my God I can scale a wall.

That's the way to live! Psalms 18 goes on like this:

> It is God who arms me with strength
>> and makes my way perfect.
> He makes my feet like the feet of a deer;
>> he enables me to stand on the heights.
>> . . . you stoop down to make me great.
> You broaden the path beneath me,
>> so that my ankles do not turn.

Verses 32, 33, 35, 36

Your little child's potential is still almost limitless. Your constant, prayerful affirmations of him will later on help him to release all that potential.

Think about father Jacob and his twelve sons. Joseph was obviously his favorite, and the other sons knew it. Is that why they turned out malicious, jealous, hating? What if they had *all* been given fancy coats, and been loved as Joseph was loved? Maybe they'd *all* have been world-ruler material like Joseph.

A child who's loved and honored grows up feeling that the sky's the limit.

17

I know a true story about little Andy and his parents in a restaurant.

"What'll you have?" said the waitress.

"I'll have a hamburger," said Andy.

"He'll have a hot dog," said his mother, and the parents gave their orders.

The waitress wrote down the parents' orders, and she looked at Andy as she wrote, and said, "One hamburger for the boy."

Andy looked after her in wonder. "She thinks I'm real!" he said.

When our first three children were tiny, Ray asked my dad for his advice on how to raise them. Daddy's only word to Ray was "Treat them like real people, real human beings."

Appreciate their feelings: "You're tired, aren't you?" "You're mad at me, aren't you?" Be compassionate.

How they need to be lifted, to be listened to, to have their opinions be considered! They may be half the height of grown-ups, but they're not half-humans! They are complete little people—in process—in their most impressionable stage. David Augsburger wrote in *Caring Enough to Comfort,*

> Sit at eye level with a child. Let your own inner child
> come out and play with the little boy or girl who is talk-
> ing to you. Listen with your eyes. Check out what

you're hearing. Find some way to affirm his or her pre-
ciousness. . . .

Listen with your eyes.

Ray was lost in the pages of a newspaper one time, and our
little Nels couldn't get his attention. Finally he bashed down the
newspaper with his hands and took hold of the two sides of Ray's
face.

"Daddy," he said, "look me right in the nose!"

18

A list of affirmations to a child can't be spouted off between 2:10 and 2:15 each afternoon. You just slip them in when you can—and as often as you can—say, up to twice a day.

What was it that God wanted to pour into the future generations of Israelis, back in the early days? The Ten Commandments. He wanted those ten concepts impressed deeply, deeply in their brains. And how did He say that it could be done?

"People," declared Moses, "let me repeat the Ten Commandments for you one last time before I die. I know they're on tablets of stone, but I want you to hear them again with your ears, all of you." And he spelled out the ten of them (Deuteronomy 5:6–21). "Now," he said,

> These commandments that I give you today are to be upon your hearts. Impress them on your children. Talk about them when you sit at home and when you walk along the road, when you lie down and when you get up.
>
> Tie them as symbols on your hands and bind them on your foreheads. Write them on the doorframes of your houses and on your gates.
>
> Deuteronomy 6:6–9

The impressions were to be put into the storage boxes of the children's subconscious minds both through their ears and through their eyes.

Through their ears, by natural family talk:

"Little Aaron, God says you must not steal."

"Deborah, God says you are always to honor us, your parents, and He promises long life to you if you do."

"Aaron, see if you can memorize these words of God: 'You shall not steal' . . . ."

Faithfully, constantly, while sitting around the house or wherever, the parents were to impress those all-important words on the children's minds—so that when dangers or temptations came, their reflex actions would automatically produce godly responses.

Second, they were to impress the children's minds through their eyes. Plaques on walls aren't so bad! Rethink the possibility of a bumper sticker. If you are too adult for visual aids, consider what they do for your children, whose subconscious minds aren't sophisticated enough yet for verbal hints and innuendos! For their sakes, and maybe even for your own, put Bibles and Christian books where they can be seen around the house.

More often than not, we assume kids understand more than they do. I have a couple of favorite stories about the unique way their little minds work—when we think they understand things the way we do, and they really have a different concept altogether.

Like the little girl taking her first ride in a plane, and sitting very tight in her seat, and finally asking her mother in a breathless voice, "When do we start getting smaller?"

Or the little boy who loved the equestrian statue of General Grant in the park. And when he was moving away, the nurse took him for one last walk through the park.

"Say good-bye to General Grant," she said.

"Good-bye, General Grant," said the little fellow.

Then as they turned away for the last time, he asked, "Who's riding on General Grant?"

Or a treasure of a story about my young friend whose daddy was sleeping on the sofa on a Sunday afternoon, and she tiptoed over and pulled up one eyelid and announced to her mother, "He's still in there."

What would we do without children? They're our favorite recreation! But in the things of eternity we must teach orally, we must teach visually, and we must teach *often*—to make sure they get the concepts right!

Commemorative stone altars were built in the Israelite days, so that when the children asked, "Daddy, what do they mean?" the answer about God's working could readily be given.

Kids love the visual! Isaiah prophesies in 44:5 that when a future generation of young Jews gets turned on to the Lord, one will say, "I belong to the Lord," and another will *write on his hand,* "the Lord's"!

You know, every town these days has a store where you can imprint T-shirts. How about a shirt for your little one: I BELONG TO JESUS. Make it size eight or so: you have to get him quick, after he learns to read and before he gets too self-conscious to wear it!

But affirmations of present status and future dreams must come from adults around the child who are forming those precious cement impressions.

It's up to you.

19

This affirming and encouraging takes time. It means being on the spot. Your child needs lots of your presence to give him all this visualizing and support!

Susannah Wesley spent one hour each day praying for her seventeen children. In addition, she took each child aside for a full hour every week to discuss spiritual matters with him or her. No wonder two of her sons, Charles and John, were used of God in their day to bring spiritual renewal to all of England and much of America!

Incidentally, would you like her six tips on child raising? Here they are:

1. Subdue self-will in a child and thus work together with God to save his soul.
2. Teach him to pray as soon as he can speak.
3. Give him nothing he cries for and only what is good for him, if he asks for it politely.
4. To prevent lying, punish no fault which is truly confessed, but never allow a rebellious, sinful act to go unnoticed.
5. Commend and reward good behavior.
6. Strictly observe all promises you have made to your child.

Or take Charles Spurgeon, one of the world's greatest English-speaking preachers. He wrote once,

I cannot tell you how much I owe to the solemn words of my good mother. It was her custom on Sunday evenings, when we were children, to stay at home with us. We sat around the table and read verse after verse, and she explained the Scriptures to us. After that there came a time of pleading and the question was asked how long it would be before we would seek the Lord. Then came a mother's prayer.

The Keswick Calendar

There is no substitute for the physical presence of parents. Six years ago I was reading an article on child raising, which said, "At home, it's the quality of time spent with the kids, not the quantity," and I wrote in the margin, "No, both!" It was gratifying to see in a recent magazine article that well-known psychologist and pediatrics specialist Dr. Lee Salk agrees with me. He writes, "It's not a matter of quantity versus quality; because children need both."

When our children were tiny, we lived in a small town with no kindergarten in the school system. You waited for first grade, and that was it. I feel good to remember that when Sherry was five and a half I could have put her in first grade, but I didn't. I loved having her at home, and I felt another year of mother-closeness was the greatest gift I could give her. So Sherry started first grade at six and a half, and so did Margie a year later. And I do believe that gave our two little girls a great deal of extra stability and extra teaching in the Scriptures, before they went off to face the "big world."

Sometimes parents force their little ones out too early because they say they're "bored at home" and need "social contacts." Is it the child or the mother who is bored with the situation? The child's cement is so wet in the preschool years! Much can be taught, and far more can be "caught."

Dr. Salk also says that day-care centers are not good for young children:

Children under the age of three are not ready for organized educational or social experiences. Up to that age
they are egocentric, crude in the expression of their emo-
tions, and not ready to play cooperatively.

And he says that three- and four-year-olds begin to benefit
from group experiences only if they are really well super-
vised.

I understand that if you're a single parent you may feel you
have no choice. Or maybe as two parents, you can't afford to
stay home; you're both forced to work to make house payments
or whatever. Dear friend, I do sympathize, and I'm praying for
you, as you read this book. But I do know that when we are
obedient to God, to do what seems right according to our understanding of His will, *He will meet our needs.* He has promised (Philippians 4:19).

Many times I remember telling adults in front of Sherry and
Margie, "We're letting them start first grade a little late. I really
enjoy having them at home; they're so much fun!" That was
surely making an impression on their young minds, that their
presence was appreciated. I have to believe that that was
deeply building security into them.

The earliest impression a child needs to have is "my mother
loves me"; "my daddy loves me." That's the prelude to "God
loves me" later on.

Armand Nicholi II wrote in *Christianity Today* (May 25,
1979),

Early family experience determines our adult charac-
ter structure, the inner picture we have of ourselves,
how we see others and feel about them, our concept of
right and wrong, our capacity to establish the close,
warm, sustained relationships necessary to have a family
of our own, our attitude toward authority and toward the
Ultimate Authority in our lives, and the way we attempt
to make sense out of our existence. No human interaction

has a greater impact on our lives than our family experience.

When I feel insecure, I can shut my eyes and feel my daddy's big hands over my two little ones in the bathroom, and it is easy to know that God loves me very much. It took time for Daddy to be with his tiny daughter every morning. But I was wet cement, and it was attitude shaping and life shaping for me.

Nicholi goes on to say,

> If any one factor influences the character development and emotional stability of an individual, it is the quality of the relationship he or she experiences as a child with *both* parents.
>
> Conversely, if people suffering from severe nonorganic emotional illness have one experience in common, it is the absence of a parent through death, divorce, a time-demanding job, or for other reasons. A parent's inaccessability, either physically, emotionally, or both, can profoundly influence a child's emotional health.

When our three children were all in high school, a doctor phoned me on a Thursday morning and asked if we'd like to adopt a baby! He was on his way to the hospital to deliver the child and needed a home for him or her—and he had to know by the next day!

Well, Ray and I were forty-one and forty—(on the ragged edge!)—but all five of us were truly thrilled with the idea of stretching our love to include a little brother or sister. By Thursday afternoon, we knew he was a boy; by Friday we had told the doctor *yes;* and that left Saturday to remember after fifteen years what babies need, so I could go shopping.

So what did I buy? All I bought was at-home clothes for me! I figured the dear people of our church would chip in on supplies, and they really did! Ray announced the big news in Sunday-evening church service, and by Monday morning, when we went to the hospital for our new baby, we had diapers, nighties, shirts, receiving blankets—enough to bring him home. Those people were wonderful! And we still had the big laundry basket that our other babies had first slept in when we were early-married-poor, so Nels had a place to sleep right away.

But in those recent years I'd started running around quite a bit, and the point of adjusting for me was to think of another five-year period in my life to be quiet at home. So I sloughed off a lot of busywork that others could do, to be close to one more little human being. And I counted on many more years after that to go half-speed, so I'd be home before and after school.

It's awesome to me. I had no idea that a public career would develop for me after raising the fourth child. But He knew there would be plenty of time for me to be "fulfilled," with the gifts and abilities He would give.

Here's another quote from Armand Nicholi:

> Parents today often resent children because they interfere with their "fulfillment." If a woman of 25 with two children, two years apart, gives full time to rearing them until they are eighteen, this leaves her with two-thirds of her adult life to follow whatever interest she desires. Is this too great a sacrifice?

Is Nels secure today? He is. At the moment Ray and I are speaking at a missionary conference in the Rocky Mountains, and as soon as we arrived and Nels found the teenagers were about to take off on a three-day backpacking trip, he attached himself to the kids and went along.

Fifteen years ago, as a newborn, when he was wet cement, he discovered Daddy and Mother liked having him around. And we affirmed this in words over and over: "Nels, it's so neat to have you in our family! You are such a pleasure to us!"

So now he assumes that others will like having him around, too—and they do.

Armand Nicholi also pointed out that a recent study in a small

USA community shows that the average time per day that fathers spend with their very young sons is about *thirty-seven seconds!*

And yet "the best gift a father can give to his son is the gift of himself."

20

When your child is close enough to you, he can be exposed to your adult life, and this is how he eventually learns to be an adult. He must be close enough, then, to be very aware of what you do. If you sit and read a book all day to little Mike, he won't watch you clean the house—and he needs to.

The four stages of discipling taught in seminars now are also the four stages of handling children:

Stage One.   You do it all, while your disciple watches.

Stage Two.   You do most of it; your disciple is starting to do some, too—but under your supervision.

Stage Three.   Your disciple is doing most of it; you're still in charge.

Stage Four.   You've backed out of the picture altogether. Your disciple is doing it all; and meanwhile he's pulled a new disciple alongside of him, and Stage One has started over again.

Through the means of the human family, this is God's method for teaching people to function on this earth. First comes Stage One, when the new babe is helpless in the crib, and mother *does it all.* (Boy, does she!)

Discipling is simply life affecting life—and after a couple of years of watching, the little one starts copying: walking, talking, taking lids off jars, and so forth.

By Stage Three the youngster is a capable teenager with lots of skills, but still under the parents' supervision.

Finally he's out of the nest and parents a child of his own, and the process starts over. These four stages are the way your child learns to cook; they're the way he learns to drive a car. They must also be the way he learns to love God, to have good table manners, to worship.

I get unhappy seeing children isolated too much.

When company comes for dinner, if they're always shunted to the kitchen or the television, how will they learn company manners? How will they learn graciousness? What will they have missed, not hearing good adult conversations?

When children are shunted off to "children's church," how will they see their parents worship? How will they learn reverence and praying and singing to God?—just from each other, or from one teacher up front? Oh, no! They need to be right at their parents' side, to copy, the way they learn to cook or drive a car. Their cement needs to be impressed by their own parents and by all the other godly adults in the church in their acts of praising and worshiping God. At least from kindergarten age on, don't let them miss all that fabulous exposure.

Over and over in the Bible we see that the children were right there when spiritual and national crises and victories came to their parents. When enemies threatened to overrun Judah, for instance, "The people of Judah came together to seek help from the Lord . . ." (2 Chronicles 20:4), and verse 13 says that "All the men of Judah, with their wives and children and little ones, stood there before the Lord." The children were exposed to the danger, to the calling on the Lord, and to the victory! They saw it all.

What might have happened differently if our little friend Lori hadn't been sitting with her parents recently in church? She wrote Ray, her pastor, a note afterward to tell him about it:

> . . . [Your sermon] talked about how to be a Christian and what a Christian is. And that single day I invited God into my heart.

Thank you for being a really neat pastor as you are.
I love God more. I am closer to him. God is in my heart
to stay. Thank you for doing that surmun. Probably more
people cam closer to God.

Love, your friend LORI.
Kisses X X X X X X Hugs O O O O O O O

Lori was in church—and it was God's moment for her new
birth. And she was in church *because her parents were in
church;* she was at their side, copying what they were doing.

Abraham "pitched his tent . . . and built an altar to the Lord,"
says Genesis 12:8. No wonder a few chapters later we find his
son Isaac *building an altar and calling on the name of the Lord*
(26:25). That's not surprising; he'd seen his father do it: that's
how he learned.

Sometimes we smile when we hear children parrot spiritual
words they've heard adults say—and we know they don't understand the implications. I don't mind. They grow up repeating what they've heard; but it's the prelude to their one day
speaking from their own reality.

All little Samuel could say to God at first were the words old
Eli told him to say: "Speak, Lord, for your servant is listening"
(1 Samuel 3:9, 10). It was pure parroting, but God didn't mind.
And Samuel grew up to be a great mouthpiece for God.

I must say, though, I had to chuckle one time when Ray was
baptizing by immersion, and a really *little* child was baptized.
Normally it would have been against the rules, but the whole
family had been converted and were being baptized together,
and it seemed wrong to leave her out—especially because she
really had received the Lord into her little heart.

Before the immersions, though, each one was to give a testimony; and this little one piped up in her five-year-old voice, "I
accepted Jesus into my heart when I was three years old, and
He changed *my whole life!*"

21

They're wet cement; the impressions are crucial. It's the time for family devotions.

It seems to me most families fall off the horse one way or the other: they don't have any family worship at all, or they make it such a big deal, it's oppressive.

I appreciate Daddy Ray's rule: "Short children, short devotions; longer children, longer devotions"! When our first three were very tiny, we read no Scripture at all. We told a short, vivid Bible story with plenty of action in it and had a little prayer.

Or we sang an action song about Jesus.

Or we memorized a short verse.

But we didn't do *all* of these *every* day.

As they grew, we read a little simple Scripture; with Nels the Living Bible had come along, and that was great.

Or we shared a little of how the Lord had helped us in our lives that day.

Or we sang a hymn together, or memorized a verse.

Sometimes Ray prayed, sometimes Mother, sometimes a child; only on leisurely mornings did we all pray. In the beginning we led our children sentence by sentence, to teach them to pray. Later sometimes we said the Lord's Prayer in unison as a family.

Variety was the key. The format was never the same two days

in a row. And we ended at the first sign of restlessness.

When they grew, we read slightly longer Scripture passages, and stopped to explain words or meanings.

We went through Kenneth Taylor's *Devotions for the Children's Hour.* For "systematic theology," children's style, we went through Donald Grey Barnhouse's *Teaching the Word of Truth.* There are lots of other good helps published. Nels made a notebook with comments and drawings from his studies in the Barnhouse book.

Who's to lead in family devotions? Father, if he will. Or father and mother together, or taking turns. Or otherwise mother alone or father alone.

Just so it happens! Tomorrow's world must learn early to worship, to handle the Word, to pray. Prepare for that Time when Jesus shall reign—

    And infant voices shall proclaim
    Their early blessings on His name!

22

But you may have a child on your mind whom you're concerned about, and you're not his parent. He hasn't had the benefit of two parents, or of the close proximity of one parent; or his parents are losers, or he has so many brothers and sisters that he's sort of lost in the shuffle, or—you know. For some reason he's been shortchanged, and you're concerned.

Move into his life all you can. A young housewife was grieving to me recently that her little neighbor has working parents who don't give him much time or emotional support, and he's beginning to have a terrible time in school.

"Karen," I said, "the Lord's given you a concern for that little boy. And he needs you."

"I know," said Karen. "That's just been dawning on me, and I'm really excited about it. He comes over almost every afternoon. I'm going to start giving him lots of hugs, and I'm going to tell him his hair is pretty, and I'm proud of his posture, and anything else I can think of."

Little Marco is wet cement.

Timothy, in Acts 16:1, had a father who was an unbeliever, but the apostle Paul gave him time and love—and look how he turned out! (Read 1 Timothy 4:12–14.)

23

And hug and kiss your child! Every human being is "skin-hungry"! Don't just do it when (or if) he asks for it; from birth on—

Hug and kiss him through his babyhood.
Hug and kiss him through his childhood.
Hug and kiss him through his teens.
Hug and kiss your grown children every chance you get.

I told my tiny Nels over and over, "You have the most kissed ears in Pasadena." Now he's over six feet tall, and when I pray with him as he goes off to sleep, sometimes I playfully pull the covers down and give his ear a smack and tell him, "You've got the most kissed ears in Corona del Mar." I've told him, "You have the most kissed ears in Africa. . . ." "You have the most kissed ears in Afghanistan. . . ." (He's been with us lots of places.)

We were in Belgium for a week when Nels was eleven, and we stayed in a home where the family knew no English and we knew no French! It was wonderful, and we got along quite well.

We went with them to their pretty little country church on Sunday: Mama, Papa, and their ten-year-old boy. Everywhere the boy went among the people, before and after church service, he automatically put his face up and got kissed. What a secure way to grow up! What a wonderful imprint in wet cement: "Adults love me. The people of my church love me." We almost wished our boy were Belgian.

Not that hugging and kissing is always easy. Not that they're always huggable and kissable! Often we have to crash through a pain barrier to do it, don't we! I'm a parent. I know the feeling.

I have in front of me a greeting card that shows a mamma porcupine with her two porcupine children stopped in front of a sign saying, "Have you hugged your kid today?" Inside, the card shows mamma with wounds all over her tummy, and the kids are wearing wicked grins!

Whatever the risk, Ray has told our children, including our sons, "Look, I'm gonna hug you and kiss you until you punch me in the mouth."

Well, they're thirty-three, thirty-two, thirty-one, and fifteen —and nobody has yet.

A Project for You

Get together some of your favorite young parents, and discuss answers to these questions in the light of affirmations:

1. How can we prepare a child for the arrival of a new baby brother or sister?

2. What if a particular twosome of our children just don't get along?

3. Is there a place for comparisons between children? For instance, can we praise one and encourage the other to copy him in a particular area?

4. What are the problems of the single child, and how can they be overcome?

5. What are the problems of the oldest child, and how can they be overcome?

6. What are the problems of the middle child, and how can they be overcome?

7. What can parents do in their own relationship which will set an example for the children?

24

Of course there have to be a couple of chapters on discipline and punishment. If you're a parent you've been waiting for that, haven't you! It isn't the prerogative of the grandparent or uncle or friend to punish; but every parent must realize that if all the child ever hears is "you're wonderful," in no time he'll be an obnoxious brat. And he'll be obnoxious at fifteen and forty and eighty-five!

When Jeremiah was made a prophet, God told him, "See, today I appoint you over nations and kingdoms to uproot and tear down, to destroy and overthrow, to build and to plant (Jeremiah 1:10).

Positive and negative: both. A garden takes more than soil and sunshine and fertilizer and water; you also have to pull weeds. A child needs more than affirmation; his sins have to be dealt with. Yes, *sins;* it's still a good word.

My daddy affirmed me; he was my sunshine and water. And, boy, did my mother pull weeds! And do you know, I loved one as much as the other.

But when I sinned, I could expect to get it! If Mother hadn't consistently "lowered the boom" on me, I would have gotten insecure. And I would have gotten confused about right and wrong.

Al and Pat Fabrizio spell out the struggle over discipline we all go through in *Children: Fun or Frenzy?*

Proverbs 22:15 says, *"Foolishness is bound in the heart of a child, but the rod of correction shall drive it far from him."*

Oh, but Lord, you surely don't mean I am to use a rod, a stick, on my child. (My first thought is, "What am I to be, a policeman with a stick to keep him in line?" I love him too much to want to hurt him.)

"He that spares his rod hates his son; but he that loves him is diligent to discipline him" (Prov. 13:24)

Then I argue, "But there are other ways of discipline. Words can be rods . . . the scolding, the rebuke."

"Withhold not correction from the child, for if you beat him with a rod, he shall not die. You shall beat him with the rod and shall deliver his soul from hell" (Prov. 23:13, 14).

"But I want to let him grow up free, without inhibitions."

"The rod and reproof give wisdom: but a child left to himself brings his mother shame" (Prov. 29:15).

But I am tempted to say, "Surely these little disobediences are not serious enough yet. He is so young. I will wait until he is older and I can reason with him and he can understand more."

"Chasten your son while there is hope, and let not your soul spare for his crying" (Prov. 19:18).

"But I am afraid if I discipline him he will only rebel more."

"Correct your son, and he will give you rest; yes, he shall give delight unto your soul" (Prov. 29:17).

The Bible version may be old—but the meaning is clear. Certainly the Bible is not talking about child abuse, which is a terrible thing. But the enemy of our souls would love to keep us distracted by extremes, so that we shy away from the specific thing God tells us to do.

"While there is hope"? What do you long for your child to be? There's still time. He's still wet cement.

25

In fact, he's not just wet cement; you might think of him as a lump of mud.

"Oh, come on, now!" you say. "You may be talking about *your* kid, but not mine!"

Well, I mean it in the finest sense. I mean it the way a sculptor would mean it.

God started with mud, or clay—and shaped Adam—the most perfect human being, except Christ, ever to walk on the earth. And He says in Jeremiah 18 that He's still shaping us as a potter or a sculptor shapes clay.

And as a sculptor starts with a shapeless mass of mud, that's sort of how a parent starts with a child. And then we're given about twenty years or so to turn that little "mass" into a social being who can make use of a rest room, say *please* and *thank you,* control his temper, use a knife and fork, blow discreetly when his nose runs. . . . All these things make him, at least in Western culture, a civilized human being.

And beyond turning him into a social being, we must pray and love and agonize until he becomes a spiritual being as well. How will it all happen?

Well, it takes lots of time and energy: physical energy, emotional energy, spiritual energy. And don't misquote me out of context, but just for this chapter alone, please indulge me a little while I say, in the light of Jeremiah 18, just think of him as a lump of mud. Then shape him!

God began with clay. He said, "Let us make man in our image
..." (Genesis 1:26), and He fashioned Adam. Through the Fall,
through the law, through the cross, through the giving of the
indwelling Holy Spirit—right up to the final experience of
heaven itself—God is in the process of shaping that mud into a
son of God like unto *the* Son of God, noble and perfect at the
last.

Now, on a very small scale, you also begin with a little lump
of clay God gives you. You're to be the sculptor.

There's Christ over there, posing for you, perfect and glori-
ous. Now, keep looking back and forth. Constantly read the
Scriptures, to get a good picture of how Christ is. Then how is
your child?

You see a lump stick out on little Mike. There's no lump like
that on Jesus. Then you must smooth it off (or pound it off) or
however—but *get it off.* For several decades you keep working
and pounding and smoothing.

You and your neighbor are conversing over a cup of
coffee. Little Mike barges into the middle of the conversation and begins to talk to you in a loud voice. You look up at
the Lord Jesus. Does He intrude? Does He force His way? Is
He loud and rude? No. Well, you want Mike to be like Him,
so you say, "Hush, Mike, later," and go on talking to your
neighbor.

But suppose the lump doesn't come off that easily, and Mike
sets up a wail or goes right on talking? Act, parent, now! Get
that lump off! The cement is wet—or, as we're saying in this
chapter—the clay is wet; the temperature is right; this is the
moment, not next time. The conditions won't be as good later;
he'll be a little more set in the wrong way.

You look him in the eye: "Mike, dear, don't interrupt when
we're talking. If you speak again, I'll spank you. As soon as we're
through, then you talk."

Assume he'll obey, turn back to the neighbor, and resume
your conversation. If he interrupts now—whoppo. One quick
spank. Knock off the lump quickly. Jesus doesn't have one, so

neither must Mike. You are helping him be conformed to Jesus' image.

Let's assume that Mike is patient and waits. End your conversation in just a sentence or two, and then turn to him with your full attention: "Mike, I'm so proud of you for waiting. You're such a good boy. Now, what did you want to say?"

If you had considered him an adult, along with your neighbor (with the right to interrupt as adults sometimes do and get away with it), you'd have misjudged him, and pretty soon he'd turn from mud to monster.

Children are really relieved to be treated as children. They can't stand the responsibility of adulthood yet. Sometimes you may not choose to explain your reason for dealing with him in a certain way. Many times when children ask, "Why can't I do so-and-so?" the best answer is, "Because I'm your mother [or father], and I say you can't." This puts all the pressure on the parent, who is bigger and stronger and ought to have to take it!

How do you know how to judge the severity of punishment? Don't judge by the act's inconvenience to you. If what he's doing is pure childishness that will pass away (spitting, playing in the toilet—things that mostly annoy only you), take it easy. If what he's doing is the seed of adult sin (defying your word, lying, and so forth), punish; get it out.

This isn't harshness; this is love—tough love. How do you sculpt a thing? Not by forever kissing and patting it! By *working* it, shaping, gouging, wetting, remaking.

Proverbs 19:18 is so strong about disciplining your child that the New International Version says that otherwise you're being a willing party to his death!

His feelings are not the most important factor. If Christ's feelings on the cross had been the most important, how could the Father ever have let His Son be crucified? But the Father knew the great principle that sin and pain go together, and Christ was assuming the payment for our sin.

It is crucial for any child to learn that there is no sin without pain. If his sin is consistently accompanied by pain, he'll begin to try to avoid sin!

26

But there's another side to this sculptoring.

The sculptor is putting his time, energy, creativity, initiative, *himself* into this thing, because he loves it. He could be out selling cars. No, he's doing what he wants to do; and sometimes he doesn't even work on it, he just stands around admiring it.

This is an essential element in handling children. Your child longs, just as you do, to know how he's doing—whether he's making it or not as a person. After all, he's the only one he's got! If all he hears is correcting, he will figure he's not making it.

In between the molding and the shaping, do lots of admiring:

"Mike, you're so cute. You look just like your dad, and I love you both."

"Todd, let me look at you. My, you're growing so big and tall! I'm so proud of you!"

"Thank you for picking up your toys, Mary. I'm a lucky mother to have you."

"How did you draw that boat so well? I'll bet I didn't draw half that well when I was your age."

I have some old notes dated May, 1961—!—for a talk I was giving to some young mothers on encouraging and affirming children. At this time our three were fourteen, thirteen, and twelve. I described affirmations for the tiny ones, and then my notes say this:

Now my children have come into the age of reasoning, so my compliments can go a step further.

"Sherry, you're a darling. I love the way you're quick to obey. That's the reason we had to do all that spanking when you were younger, Honey, and look how it's paid off!"

"Margie, you're just lovin' size. What did I ever do to deserve such a sweet little girl?"

"Buddy, you're still in the blossoming stage, but I know you don't mind my spanking you now and then, do you? Because I really see improvement in you all along, and I pray for you, and I think if I'm just faithful to punish you now and then when you need it, these next couple of years, you'll really mature into a fine young person, all out for Christ, and then I can just relax and you'll be on your own."

When I read these old notes today, I can't believe how kind God has been.

Sherry was so strong-willed, she *did* need lots of spanking! Today that will is channeled into loving God with all her heart, studying zealously for the Bible-conference speaking and Bible-class teaching which she loves—and steadily, unswervingly, joyfully, loving her husband and two little girls.

Margie heard that phrase all her childhood: "You're just lovin' size!" Now she's a capable wife and mother of two girls and a boy, guiding her house well, and supporting wholeheartedly John, her pastor-husband.

And Bud has surely matured into a "fine young man, all out for Christ"! He is totally committed to the Lord, to his wife Jani, to his two little sons and tiny daughter, as he teaches Greek and Hebrew and is assistant pastor in a wonderful church.

Here's another paragraph in those May, 1961, notes:

To me, it's as wicked to withhold the praise as the punishment. Pity the poor youngster who just gets hollered at all day! The majority of the time our children

should know they are our *great delight*—and then the
minute they disobey, whammo: apply the punishment,
get the sin paid for, and then they can be our great
delight again.

Why is it so important to affirm a child? Because a child who
is truly accepted by his parents and/or influencing adults can
grow up learning to accept himself. Without a constant, debili-
tating sense of guilt and defeat, he will become at ease with
himself. He'll be able to admit his own failures and weaknesses.
He'll be able to forget himself and love others. He won't spend
his energies worrying about what people think of him, and he
won't spend his energies putting down others.

"Fathers," says Ephesians 6:4, "do not exasperate your children; instead, bring them up in the training and instruction of
the Lord."

"Bring them up. . . ." Catch the word, *up!*
Wonderful!

A Project for You

*Before you continue reading this book, this ought to be the
time for you to have a period of quiet.*

1. First, talk to God about the child or children in your life.
   Pray for yourself as a parent and/or model. Pray for their
   development and their future. And ask Him to give you
   wisdom in knowing how to affirm them.

2. Read again Deuteronomy 6:6–9.

3. What should you impress on them through their *ears?*
   Write a list of affirmations for your child. If you have several
   children, the list may be the same; or one or two things may
   be unique for each child.

4. What should impress on them through their *eyes?* Moses
   suggested something on their bodies to wear, and something on their house, to remind them continually of God's
   commandments

27

I was talking to Dorothy, one of the most conscientious young mothers I've ever seen. She made an appointment with me to tell me how she was raising her five children, and I was impressed. She's a modern Susanna Wesley—with time for each one, goals for each one, schedules for each one, Bible study and prayer times for each one, music lessons for each one, athletic projects for each one, family devotions together, family social times together, family educational trips together.... It wore me out just listening to it all! But it really was good. I watched how her children sat stiffly on chairs among the adults as long as they were told to, and when they were released, they ran off to play as wildly as any normal kids.

"What plan do you have to release them gradually as they grow up?" I asked her.

She looked a little startled.

"I mean, when they're in their twenties and thirties, will you still have them on the same regimen?"

"Of course not," she said. "They'll be married, and have their own kids. . . ."

"Then you need a program for transition," I said. "Your tight hold works wonders now, but that oldest one is ten, and in a couple of years, if your hold on her doesn't start to loosen, she'll begin to rebel. And she ought to. She'd have no other way to grow up and out of the nest."

This young mother was so teachable and humble! I loved her. "What do you suggest?" she said.

I showed her that her program was great so far—but that she must not act as if the job were forever.

We looked at what happened to Jesus at the age of twelve (Luke 2:41–52). You remember that He went with Joseph and Mary to the temple and then lingered behind when they left, asking questions of the teachers.

When His parents found Him, Mary chided, "Son, why have you treated us like this? Your father and I have been anxiously searching for you."

"Your father and I"! In twelve years it had become very comfortable to think of Joseph as Jesus' father.

And you'd think Jesus would have been even more sure of it, when for all His life everyone around Him had assumed it to be true. But no: He was twelve years old. He was beginning to move from total dependence on human relationships to His own unique relationship with God.

"Why were you searching for me?" He asked. "Didn't you know I had to be in my Father's house?" (v. 49).

"My Father"! He didn't mean Joseph. And even though He went on home with them and was still obedient to them, He had put a little distance between Him and them. He was growing away from His earthly parents and growing toward His heavenly Parent.

Encourage this. As you see your child growing through adolescence, start backing off a little—the speed at which you do it not depending on your own schedule, but on his development.

Start saying, "Stevie, now you have to do what *I* tell you, but later on you'll be doing what *God* tells you. That'll be better. I make mistakes, but He doesn't!"

Be telling him for years that this is going to happen. It's great psychology! It produces the effect of "don't leave me yet, Mother," instead of "isn't this woman ever going to get off my back? How do I get out from under her?"

When does the shift-over begin to happen? Of course it's very gradual, but perhaps around the age of twelve, the age of Bar Mitzvah.

Watch for him to start being God-directed (Luke 2:49), and then start backing off. From twelve to perhaps twenty, maybe longer, give him supportive, loving withdrawal. Make the affirmations less obvious but just as constant during this period. They were never more needed. There will be rocky periods along the way.

When he reverts to childishness—if the issue is big enough to be worth it—you revert to total control. When he surges ahead in periods of more maturity, back off and admire him exceedingly—and give him his head. But always have withdrawal in mind, and explain what you're doing.

Let him know, "Mike, the more I sense you're getting your orders from God, the less I'll tell you what to do. And I'm thoroughly delighted to hand you over to Him. Soon my job will be all done, and you'll just be following Him, and we'll be good friends. I'll be so proud of you!"

Dorothy and I talked about this together, and she said to me, "I have an idea. My husband and I have always made goals for the children on their birthdays."

(Let me interject that I didn't comment on this to Dorothy, but that seems a bad plan to me. The intimation is then that the goal must be reached within a twelve-month period, before the next birthday, and puts the child under the pressure of the parents' set rate of development, not his own natural pace.)

Dorothy went on, "Wouldn't it be good if beginning with their twelfth birthdays, they made their own goals?"

"Excellent!" I applauded.

Oh, how we have to build humility into parenting! How we must decrease, that He may increase! And especially from age twelve on, we have to give them room to breathe, to move around, to be creative, to be responsible, to begin to make their own decisions.

Harry N. Zelinka, district director of the Family Service of Los Angeles, comments in *Prime Time* magazine, "The purpose

of being a parent is to prepare one's child to leave home."
Charles Swindoll writes in *You and Your Child,*

> Wise, sensitive parents spend years helping their children
> reach their full potential. This does two things, both of which
> are healthy and wholesome. First, it helps the parent loosen the
> ties. Month by month, year after year, as the process occurs the
> parent is releasing—slowly but surely. . . .
>
> Secondly, it helps the youngster stretch his wings without
> fear of getting them clipped. A context of secure, loving free-
> dom is his to enjoy. He's eager to become himself as a person.
> He's not made to feel guilty because he enjoys the process.
>
> And when the final day of release arrives, he's ready and so
> are his parents. Tears may flow—but those are joyful tears!

Or, as a cartoon in front of me shows, the mamma dog is
standing in front of her litter of pups, and with both a grin and
a tear in her eye, she's saying:
"The time has come for each of you to find a little boy to
follow home."

28

Parenting a teenager, and/or effectively discipling one, means you have to grow up yourself. It leads you into deep waters, deeper than you've ever experienced. How I pray for sponsors of high-school groups in churches, and youth ministers! They will not be effective unless they go far, far beyond the cokes and jokes.

Don't say, "Well, when they're teenagers, they're going to be rebellious for a while." I remember friends of my parents who said, "No doubt our teenagers will go over fool's hill for a while like the rest"—and they did, with much heartache and damage. My parents said, "They don't have to; ours won't." They said it in front of us, too—and none of the four of us ever did.

How much control, how much release? Oh, how hard it is to know! Usually parents of teenagers work harder on the control than on the release—which probably encourages their rebellion. Both are needed in huge amounts, but I really believe if we made the release the more openly emphasized part, they would take better to the control.

Expect God to speak differently to them than He does to you. They are being prepared for a later world you and I won't ever be a part of; His plans for them are specialized. Let them go— and understand that you cannot follow.

Each of our grown children's theology has taken just a slightly different bent from Ray's and mine. Well, God has places for each of them to go and things for them to do that are not for us. We can trust His shapings.

God will not just repeat to your children what He said to you. They are not clones. Relax. Let God lead them, and back them up.

Gideon was a young fellow who had a mind-blowing encounter with the Angel of God (Judges 6:11). He wanted to respond, but he was afraid of his parents' reaction.

Well, eventually he obeyed God, anyway—and shocked the whole town. *But his father defended him against them all* (v. 31).

Yea! Three cheers for his father! And so Gideon was released in his spirit to be the mightiest tool for God of his day.

That father must have been terrific at both control and release. Gideon and his brothers are described in this way: "Each one had the bearing of a prince" (8:18).

29

Affirmations for your teenagers are absolutely a must. When they seem the most obnoxious (like having the telephone receiver glued to the ear and explaining, "I'm *not* talking to him any more; we're just waiting to see who hangs up first")—or when their humor is the dumbest ("No wonder I'm confused: one of my parents was a man and the other was a woman"), that's when they need affirmations the most.

They need to know you're listening, when the rare times come around that they have the courage to talk—about how to face the future, about their friends, about their pressures, about school, sex, loneliness, and God. . . .

They need to know you're still on the same old ground with them—communicating their needs for family, church, responsibility, and wholesomeness—that you haven't changed.

They need a sense of direction, and of balance in their lifestyle. Everything often seems out of whack to them.

They need your understanding and support through all their physical woes: tooth decay and acne and hormonal changes. One large survey of adolescents reported in *Changing Times* found abnormalities of heart and blood vessels in one out of twenty; nearly half had heart murmurs, and 13 percent had high blood pressure.

And they need to hear from you *words*. Choose your own

affirmations, of course, according to your teenager. But they may include,

1. "You're making wiser decisions these days."
2. "You're maturing so wonderfully!"
3. "You're beginning to face the world with courage."
4. "You are better able to relax now and feel comfortable with situations."
5. "Your mind is sharper for your studies."
6. "You really, basically, love people!"
7. "I see that you love the Lord more and more."
8. "You really enjoy school."
9. "You're beginning to finish more things that you start."
10. "You're more organized now."
    And for the future:
11. "You're going to pick a wife [husband] so carefully."
12. "You're going to be a wonderful parent."
13. "You're going to have a wonderful effect on the world for God."

Are you saying, "Those affirmations sure don't apply to my kid"? Well, remember Step One is prayer—strong crying to God for that child of yours.

And Step Two is putting it into his mental storage box. And it's affirming him *ahead of schedule:* supporting him (as God does us) with descriptions of his future self. Slip them in as often as you can—but in moments when they seem the most—not the least—believable!

And always, through every stage, "I love you, and I'm so proud of you." And another thing: let most of your affirming be with no one else around, and accompanied, when possible, by hugs and pats.

Nels is fifteen, and the last three or four years I've been saying, "I'm going to enjoy it when you can drive our car. You'll be a good driver—sharp and courteous. It'll be neat."

Now he has his learner's permit, and he's already proud of being a good driver—sharp and courteous. And it *is* neat.

"*Train a child in the way he should go*" (Proverbs 22:6): in the specific, unique way God leads you to envision for that particular child.

("You're going to make people around you so warm and happy, Charlie; you have a great personality.")

("I'm so glad you love to pray, Michele; all your life you'll find God drawing closer and closer to you as you draw closer and closer to Him.")

". . . and when he is old," the Proverb goes on to say, "he will not turn from it."

The impression on the wet cement will have become firm and clear.

A Project for You

Do you "admire" well? Most people need to strengthen their "admiring" muscle.

1. Spend some time in prayer right now, admiring the Lord. Don't thank Him for things; just tell Him in what ways He's wonderful.

2. Admire the adults around you today: your spouse, your roommate, your business associate, your friend. They all need it; they all hurt for it.

3. Admire the children around you today. Admiring adults— honestly, sincerely—will rectify some serious defects; but admiring children will shape tomorrow's world of people.

When you say to a child, "Thank you for being my friend," you are modeling relational warmth. You are helping a little person learn to open up and become comfortable with love and loving expressions. Who knows what he may become as an adult?

When you say, "You have the prettiest hair . . .", you are helping him gain confidence in his appearance. Someday he may do business before kings. . . .

Dr. Clyde Narramore tells about one of the most successful and loved schoolteachers in greater Los Angeles, whom he sought out one day to discover her secret.

"I make a habit of saying one good thing about every child in my class, every day," she said.

Then she sighed. "I almost missed one today. Scottie was so bad, I couldn't think of one good thing to say all day. Finally, just now as he was running out to go home, I said to him, 'Scottie, you have the bluest eyes. . . .' "

30

Let's back up to see that there are three basic ways to handle youngsters from toddler to young adulthood: SHAPE UP, PULL UP, and LIFT UP; and for these three terms I'm heavily indebted to my friend Sally Folger Dye.

You know the shape-up approach well: "You do what I say, or I'll do so-and-so"—some kind of threat. This approach is simple, frontal, understandable, and it's used constantly by parents, spouses, schoolteachers, and many others.

Indeed, as far as I see it, it's the *best* approach for the tiny child receiving his first "no-nos." "Shape up; obey what I say; or else I will do something you don't like." It gives clear choices to a child of right and wrong, with painful results if he chooses the wrong.

"*Shape up,* or there'll be trouble." It's simple. It's elementary. Many parents never shift out of the shape-up approach—but the truth is, the more the child grows, the less satisfactory this method is. The more he matures, the more degrading the shape-up approach becomes. It speaks of one-upmanship and condemnation. It implies superiority on the part of the adult, and that just decimates a young person. Implications of his inferiority are just too much: his own conscience and his natural insecurity are both already condemning him; and more criticism just makes him more and more desperate.

Parents who keep using the shape-up approach, says Sally

Dye, "don't usually notice its negative effects until the teenage years, when the children learn to join the duel and turn the shape-up attitude back on them." And duel it becomes—with the children denying and masking their guilt, and shouting louder and louder, as they try to turn the blame on the parents. And the bigger the child, the less feeling of control the adult has at this point, so pretty soon the kid's heat is matched by the adult's. Oh, having raised four children, this whole scene is very familiar to me!

The second technique is pull up: when the adult deliberately and unemotionally determines a goal and patiently helps the child by pulling him up toward that goal.

This is an excellent way to handle elementary-school children, who love goals, projects, and rewards. This is Boy and Girl Scout approach, with their pins and merit badges: "We are setting for you a worthwhile goal of lighting a fire with two matches (or hiking so many miles); and if you achieve this, we will all applaud you and give you a reward."

This is exactly what my friend Dorothy was doing, setting goals for each of her five children's birthdays—physical, educational, cultural, and spiritual—and working with them day and night until each one of them got there.

31

But now take a look at the third method—a wonderful treasure of a technique not used often enough.

By the lift-up approach, according to Sally Dye, "The counselor takes a vulnerable position 'under' the counselee and lifts him toward his own personal goal, not the counselor's goal. No matter how much training and experience the counselor has, he chooses to take this humble attitude, speaking like an adult [to one] he loves and respects. In a sense the uplifter refuses the status of counselor."

I have noticed in the last several years how responsive to me and to my wishes Nels has been when I've treated him as my equal—no, my superior. From about his twelfth birthday on, when I could, I asked his advice. I leaned on him. I asked him to help me because I needed his superior wisdom or skill. I deliberately confided my insecurities and problems to him (not deep ones), referred to his father as "Ray" in an adult-to-adult sort of confidentiality, and asked him to pray for me concerning this or that weakness on my part. When we walk together, sometimes I take his arm, as I would a grown-up's. And sometimes I kiddingly call him "you big, strong, handsome man!" to reinforce his growing inner image of himself as just that.

The results have been wonderful. Of course, he often reverts to his little-boy ways and prances around and acts foolish like a six-year-old. Good! He only has one childhood; he'd better squeeze out all he can get from it! But I also notice he's often protective of me, gentle in his care of me, and solicitous in offering me advice—often good advice that I need.

I wish I'd done it more! Teenagers eat it up. They're so anxious to become important, worthy people in this world, and they need every possible affirmation to help them get there.

But it's tricky! The young person's own inner goals are what's important here, not the parents' goals for him. And even if the child has been sensitively raised from birth, probably his own dreams won't quite coincide with his parents' dreams for him. So be it. The parent must deeply respect the personal goals of his child and help him attain them.

If his goal is "I want to quit high school and get married," then he's probably too immature yet for heavy doses of the lift-up approach.

But keep talking, those of you who handle a teenager! Keep the channels of communication open! Let him know that the more he begins to follow what God is telling him to do, the less you'll have to tell him—and that you expect that time to come soon! Explain the lift-up approach, even before you begin to use it, and explain how glad you are that, before long, his goals for himself will be God's goals for him, and you'll be doing everything you can to help him get there. *And don't equate God's goals with your goals!*

In a most amazing and mystical way, Philippians 2:3 must begin to apply to the adults around a teenager: "Do nothing out of selfish ambition or vain conceit [you're going to go this direction because it will gratify my ambitions for you!], but in humility consider others better than yourselves."

If your child is not yet there, *affirm him as if he were,* as often as it is possibly appropriate. Affirm him *ahead of schedule.* Admire him verbally, considering him better than yourself. After all, as Mr. Lincoln said, you know what you are, but who knows what this child may become?

Actually, this technique of stooping below the level of the child can begin well before the teen years. Ask his opinion. Ask his advice. It will do wonders for him:

"Teach me how to hop the way you do."

"Should I make the bed next or put away the laundry?"

"Do you think I talk too much?"

Sally Dye lists three aspects of the uplifting technique: creative hope, self-revelation, and deliberate vulnerability. And she says,

> Each one of these acts as a challenge catalyst with power enough to effect a change in the person's life position. Several catalysts working together have a powerful, life-changing effect. . . . These each work together to bring about honest confession and forgiveness that is essential before the standard and goals can be accomplished.

Creative hope, the first, is the technique of affirmations that this book has been suggesting. One of Sally's sentences especially leaped off the page at me:

> Creative hope is like the forms made ready to shape the concrete of the future habits.

There it is! *Your child is wet cement, and affirmations are the forms to mold him to his future shape.*

Oh, this is God's way! It is biblical and right. *Love always hopes* (1 Corinthians 13:7), and God's very technique for us *is* creative hope: accepting us as righteous before we ever in fact are. This is why nothing less than faith can please Him: He insists that we accept by faith and believe totally the beautiful things He says about us—long before they are actually true. Amazing and wonderful!

God has often affirmed His chosen ones ahead of actuality. He appeared to Gideon when Gideon was a young farmer, the least member of an unimportant family of the weakest clan in his hometown and said to him, "The Lord is with you, mighty warrior!" (Judges 6:12).

Sally Dye says,

On the other hand, many a spouse or child is kept from
achieving his inner standards and goals because someone close
to him insists on pointing out his weaknesses in his present
behavioral condition, rather than seeing him as progressing
towards becoming the person they both want him to become.

An esteemed professor once said to me, "This technique you
speak of is too powerful. Don't use it. I knew a mother once who
used this on her child. She wanted him to become a great
pianist. Her hope was so effective that he saw himself as that
great pianist when he became an adult, but he did not have
enough actual talent to fulfill that role!"

Here we see power misused, when the parent imposed her
own goals on the child, instead of lifting him toward his own
inner, God-given goals.

But, Sally Dye goes on to say, "The aim of creative hope, or
affirmations, is to make the goal appear more real than the
present state of inadequacy."

The second lift-up technique is *self-revelation,* when the
uplifter tells about his own weaknesses and problems in a dis-
arming way (as I've sought to do lately with Nels), for the purpose of helping him grow. To lift a heavy load effectively you
have to get underneath it, and there comes a point in the life
of a teenager when the parent (or influencing adult) has to do
the same. In effect, you lose all your authority. You say, "I know
all about your weaknesses. I have them, too."

One of the most beautiful characteristics of Ray's preaching
ministry is that he frequently says from the pulpit, "My, how I
need this for myself . . . I fall down here, too. . . . God has to help
me as well as you. . . ." And his flock's response is to identify with
him ("He's a real person just like me") and to love him!

Jesus lowered Himself to servant humility for our sakes (Philippians 2:5–8), and tells us to do the same to each other.

What happens when an adult humbles himself before a teenager? There's no more playing of games, putting on masks,
competing, wounding each other. It opens the way to honesty.

There's no longer one-way control, as when he was younger, but two-way dialogue.

And the most powerful possible result is that the young person is more apt to reveal his own needs and ask for help—and God says confession is an absolutely essential prerequisite to cleansing, renewal, and fresh starts with Him (*see* Psalm 51; Isaiah 57:15; 66:2, Acts 3:19).

Deliberate vulnerability is the key. It's embarrassing; it's a deep, hard path to follow—but it's godly and it's potent. It's beautifully described by Sally Folger Dye in this way:

> When a dog realizes it cannot win a fight, it shows its submission and surrender at the onset by lying down at the great dog's feet and baring its vulnerable throat and belly. In this position, it could get killed in an instant. The dog with the advantage has to be enraged to attack another dog who opens itself in this way. I have never seen such an attack, though I have lived in a village for years [in New Guinea] with a large number of violent dogs who do not hesitate to attack each other when they get a chance.
>
> In the same way a conscientious person takes the risk of not being able to justify his guilt if he attacks someone who has volunteered total vulnerability. Even in war, where consciences are often bitterly hardened, many stories are heard of unusual mercy to those who are purposefully and genuinely vulnerable. In such a context the humble who are actually attacked can "heap coals of fire on one's head." Apparently this is the fire of a guilty conscience (Romans 12:20).
>
> Amazing as it sounds, vulnerability is a position of power. Jesus Himself chose this position of humility to come into the world and revolutionize it (Philippians 2:5–11). He commands His disciples to do the same (Mark 9:35; 10:43–45; 8:34, 35). One-upmanship has little effect when one deliberately puts himself as low as he can get. There is nothing for the counselee to rebel against, no threatening authority, no fear of humiliation. . . .

The problem is, my friend, this attitude cannot be faked. If the adult's mind-set, deep down inside, is one of superiority, the young person will see the cover-up immediately. His very intonations of voice and words and body language will give it away, and the kid will put his own mask back on and start playing games again.

The adult has to be genuinely obedient to Christ's command to become a servant (*see* John 13:14–17). With a true servant's heart, his attitude must be that of kneeling before the young person to wash his feet, to make him whole and clean again in every part.

And his frame of mind must be so to respect the young person that he actually considers him better than himself (*see* Philippians 2:3–5; Romans 12:3–5, 16). Is this too much to swallow? Then add "at least potentially."

As I write this, Ray has just begun the fourth pastorate of his life. In this his thirtieth year of ministry, he's once again assumed a new role of leadership. Last night we sat at dinner with two dear friends and talked deeply to Rolf and Louise about the price of leadership.

"It means staying at the foot of the cross," we agreed.

Rolf, in a period of crisis in the very large business which he leads, had just had to step outside of his usual beautiful pull-up, lift-up leadership and strongly revert to shape-up. He spelled out all God was teaching him.

"Ray, I see how you commit your life to those you want to lead," said Rolf, "and then you step down in humility to shepherd them as the Lord did. Boy, that's tough, and you do it beautifully."

"And, Rolf, that's exactly what you do," said Ray. "That's why your business associates love you so much."

So the two friends did a lot of affirming of each other.

But what Rolf had just done is important for us to see. Know well that each of the three techniques is legitimate at some time or other, and be ready with your teenager to use whichever one is appropriate at the moment.

Use *lift up* as your continuing way of life, which will carry you into the years ahead when you'll be adults together, with great respect for each other.

Use *pull up* as he is still ready to receive it, gently suggesting rewards for his meeting your requests.

And then use *shape up* for the temporary emergency.

32

Much of what was said in the last chapter also applies to your relationship with your grown child.

Maybe your child is grown, but still in the nest. Sometimes a young adult has a particularly hard time getting out.

Do you have one at home like that? He's not on drugs, or sexually promiscuous, or hostile. He may lack ambition, and be unsure of himself. He may work at a job which isn't stretching, and yet he passes up opportunities for advancement. He just likes it in the nest, and he's afraid to get out.

Don't coddle him too long. Don't excuse him forever. ("He's a late bloomer," parents can say—and their kid still hasn't blossomed at forty!)

That period around the age of twelve was crucial, when you should have started preparing him for independence. Never mind; feeling guilty doesn't help. What do you do now?

Start affirming him. Myron Brenton writes in his article "When Children Won't Leave Home,"

> Parents whose adult children won't leave the nest often do the very things that will keep those children home-bound—taking care of them as if they were really young children, in a sense encouraging them to lead haphazard, irresponsible lives. Therefore, the first step for parents with adult children who are caught in a pattern of dependence

and irresponsibility is to break out of the pattern.

But take it one step at a time. Your ultimate goal might be to have the child move out, but he or she will have to build up some self-confidence first. As Ms. Kovar [Barbara P. Kovar, executive director of the Family Service of Dedham, Massachusetts] says, "You've got to help them grow up first or they'll never be able to."

Prime Time magazine

If there are two parents, act in unison; expect rental money and shared chores; allow him some privacy but expect him to conform to your value standards—and *give him words.*

Implant in his ears over and over again the picture you have of his success on his own. Describe it, expect it, be excited over it. Couch your words in all the positive, loving belief in him that God will give you, and *ask God for the same things.* Tell God, and tell your child. And make both your prayers and your affirmations full of faith in God's strong power to work on behalf of your child.

Is your adult child out of the nest—and all you dreamed he would be? Affirm him over and over; enjoy him as your dear friend. Don't tell him what to do! Don't tell his spouse what to do! Those days are over.

Is he out of the nest—and less than you dreamed he would be? In whatever way you think he is less—less intellectually, less occupationally, less physically, less socially, less spiritually —in your mind's eye, put him in your two hands, and give him over to God. *God is now assuming totally the parent role.* You are through. And He's up to it! If there are further changes to be made, He can change your child—as He can change you.

But no more criticism—not even in your prayers. Let your prayers be lifting and intercessory, but also *thank God for him just the way he is.* Is he in really bad shape? There is the unfathomable mystery of God's working which includes all He needs to do *in you,* as well as in your grown child.

Relax under His shapings and workings on you both. Ask God to cleanse from your heart all pride which makes you personally defensive or angry over his condition.

And be sure you read the last section of this book.

33

Nels said to me, "You ought to have a chapter on adopted children."

"Are you going to write it with me?" I asked.

"Sure I will," he said—but the summer passed, and now he's gone off to school. Well, I don't carry out all my good intentions, either.

We took Nels to be our boy when he was four days old, and from the beginning of our communications with him we said he was adopted. We said it when we introduced him to people, right in front of Nels; and we said it with all the thrill in our voices possible. ("Aren't we lucky? Isn't he great?") It wasn't hard, because that's what we really felt—and feel.

Nels knew he was adopted long before he understood what that meant. I remember one time he said to me, "Mamma, I'm so glad I was adopted, and that I grew in your tummy—!"

And God was kind to give him other positive impressions of being adopted, which confirmed our own. I was so grateful to Ted and Dorothy Engstrom's beautiful daughter Joanne, when as a teenager she gave little Nels a hug one day and said, "Aren't we both lucky to be adopted?"

And there was the time when the Caspersons invited us to dinner—a wonderful family in our church with eight children, some natural and some adopted. The adopted ones were of every color under the sun. At the long table some of the kids began to brag, "I'm adopted!"

"I'm adopted, too!" said little Nels, not to be outdone.

"But I'm Hawaiian!" crowed one of the little boys.

"I'm Hawaiian, too!" insisted Nels, and for a few months he told people that he was Hawaiian.

If you have adopted children, I think you'll be encouraged by Nels' contribution to this book in the third section. I had absolutely no idea what he would say—but it shows how totally he identifies with his adopted family. Praise the Lord! We love him so much, and he's such a pleasure to us.

Years ago I remember saying sometimes, "We love him just as much as the children we produced. There's no difference." I realize now that we haven't said that for years: he is so much a part of us and of the other children, there's no reason to say it. We're all part of the same "stuff."

34

All people need children in their lives!

Pastors have the great privilege of being close to children, and it's one of the reasons Ray loves to pastor. Who but a child can tickle us so inside?

Pastors have received letters like these:

> I am a good Chrischun but i can't spel and add to good. . . .

> iI read the bibel every day since I was a little KId. So far iI am up to the first page. . . .

> What is God's telephone number? I would like to call Him when I feel sad. . . .

How can you resist little people?

But for many more reasons, you need children in your life, all your life. Children can keep you from lethargy and in a condition of spiritual renewal.

It was when Enoch had Methuselah that he began to walk with God (Genesis 5:22). Often young couples are occupied with themselves until they have babies—and then they begin to form godly habits.

Conversely, when children leave the home, parents can get lazy and selfish again and fall back into bad habits. You know what midlife is: when you stop being interested in child care and start being interested in Medicare!

But no; always have a heart for the children. See that there are always young ones around you—watching you, learning from you.

And as you need children, so they need you. Children everywhere are waiting for *your* renewal and commitment and fervor.

If you're not a biological parent, how can you love and shape a child? Well, just take one into your heart and life in whatever way God leads you. Jesus said, "Whoever welcomes a little child . . . in my name welcomes me" (Matthew 18:5).

There are many ways to adopt a child. Doing it legally and giving him your name is one way. But children have been assumed by others ever since baby Moses and before; and I have a strong conviction that thousands of adults in this world need far more children than they have. They need to get next to little ones, especially the needy ones, and pour into them what natural parents are unable to give. The best of parents need extra help in the teen years, and the less than best need help from the very beginning. (This is discussed further in my book *Love Me With Tough Love.*)

One of my dear friends, a godly, wise, exciting young woman, as beautiful as a model, had parents who were total losers. When she was little, she got in the habit of stealing down the road to where her two bachelor uncles lived. They fed her the breakfast she wouldn't have gotten otherwise, prayed and read the Bible with her; helped her with her schoolwork, got her the clothes she needed, and just generally raised her. And what a good job they did! She is not only normal and free from psychological scars, she is radiant and aggressive in her love and good works.

Moses had been taken in and raised by the daughter of Pharaoh, and given a training and education and preparation for leadership he never could have received from his natural parents. So early on in his career he did the same thing: he "adopted" young Joshua and trained him to one day take his place. And Joshua's leadership was as outstanding as Moses' had been. (*See* Exodus 19:9; 24:13; Numbers 11:28; 13:8; 14:6, 30, 38; Deuteronomy 1:38; 31:7, 8; Joshua 1.)

Bad influences on children not your own are also passed on. Samuel was raised by Eli, a priest, who was a negligent father. That was the model Samuel had to look at; and a generation later, Samuel was a negligent father himself (1 Samuel 8:1–5).

Look through the Bible and see how many cases there are of young people—wet cement—who were impressed by other than their parents. Elijah took on young Elisha, who left his oxen right in the field in order to stick close to him and be his attendant (1 Kings 19:19–21). Elijah turned out to have a prickly personality but great spiritual power in his life. When it was time for Elijah to go to heaven, Elisha asked for a double portion of Elijah's spirit (2 Kings 2:9)—not for his prickly personality but for his power! And it was given to him.

Then there was Esther, an orphan raised by her uncle Mordecai. He was a wonderful man, whose influence she drew upon, not only as a girl, but even—by remote control—when she was queen of the whole empire (Esther 2:20).

Consider Joash, only seven years old when he became king of Judah. His background was terrifically bloody. His father had been killed when he was a year old, and his grandmother, to take over the throne, had tried to kill all the rest of the family —but baby Joash got snatched and hidden and guarded for six years (2 Kings 11:1–3).

The hero of the era was a wonderful priest, Jehoiada, who finally staged a coup and had the horrible grandmother killed and the child Joash crowned as king. But he didn't stop there; he guided Joash's behavior in the ways of God as long as he was alive. And 2 Kings 12:2 says that "Joash did what was right in the eyes of the Lord all the years Jehoiada the priest instructed him."

This is what discipling is all about. (Read about this further in *Love Me With Tough Love.*) Who knows the influence you can be as you affect children and young people, who are tomorrow's world? If the child you take under your wing isn't a king, he could still turn out to be kingly. Your giving him time—laughing with him, crying with him, studying with him, playing with him, urging him on to success, and backing him with your prayers—could shape one of tomorrow's great influences in the world.

Such was the influence a generation ago of Henrietta Mears, a single woman, on young Bill Bright, who is today the founder and international head of Campus Crusade for Christ.

Adopting. Discipling. Nobody who has Christ in his heart is excused from making a mark on the children around him! They're wet cement. They're ready.

> Parent birds
> Feed young nestlings
> What they can.
> Who can tell
> How high some day
> One of them
> May soar?

A Project for You

If your concern is a teenager, meet together with good friends who are also concerned about teenagers. Divide the time into discussion, writing affirmations, and prayer.

1. Read Psalms 127 and 128. Discuss control versus release, and ask advice of each other for specific situations.
    Discuss the need of your teenager for extra "parents." If you're a parent, how can these be provided? If you are one of these nonbiological parents, what are your roles and functions? Will some in the group volunteer to "adopt" temporarily others' needy teenagers?
    Discuss *shape up, pull up,* and *lift up;* learn from each other as you flesh them out in shared experiences.

2. Have a time of quiet to think through and write down a list of affirmations for your child in this period of his life.

3. Spend the last part of your session in group prayer, for each other, for the children, and for faithfulness and effectiveness in affirmations.

Section III

About Us and Ours...

35

Our children are Sherry Harrah, thirty-three, married to
Walt; Margie McClure, thirty-two, married to John; Bud (Ray,
Jr.), thirty-one, married to Jani; and fifteen-year-old Nels.

*A book about children ought to include contributions from
our own,* I thought.

Bud lives in Northern California; he's the farthest away. I
called him on the phone.

"Bud," I said, "about the book for Revell. It's about children,
you remember. Do you suppose you'd be willing to contribute
to it?"

"Oh, yes, I'd be happy to," said Bud.

"Oh, that would be neat," I said. "As far as the subject goes,
it can be about your own childhood and also, if you like, about
your raising Eric and Krista and Dane—both good and bad—
whatever the readers can learn from.

"As for format," I went on, "I've got two ideas; maybe you'll
have a better one. Each of you children could just write your
own thing, whatever you want to say. Or else we could gather
around the dining table with a tape recorder and just talk."

In my mind I was picturing the second way. Transcribed,
you'd have all those nice quotations marks and white spaces on
the page. Conversations are such easy reading.

"I'd like to write my own," said Bud.

"That would be super!" I chirped. (I should have known. Our

scholar son is a researcher; he's careful and thoughtful and thorough.)

"I wouldn't be too happy spouting off the top of my head," said Bud.

Nels was across the room as I was phoning. Afterward I said to him, "Nels, Bud's farther away, and it makes sense for him to write his own. Maybe the Southern California children—Sherry, Margie, and you—could gather around the dining table and tape it. What do you think?"

"I'd like to write my own," said Nels.

"Great," I gulped. "That'll be really good." (I should have known that, too. Our gangly fifteen-year-old is an extrovert and confident to handle any project without help!)

I phoned Sherry in Pasadena and explained the options. "The two brothers want to write their own," I said, "but you two sisters have always been so close; don't you think it would be great for us to get around the dining table?"

"Whatever you say, Mom," said Sherry. "I'm really happy to do it either way for you." That's our Sherry: capable and easy to live with.

Then Ray and Nels and I were leaving for conference speaking, so Sherry agreed to ask Margie. Of course Margie wanted to tape it. She's a sparkling personality and very verbal. (Boy, I'm making "mother noises," aren't I!)

So evolved this next section. But before I turn it over to the children. . . .

36

I got into mothering fast. Ray was a twenty-two-year-old college senior—older because he'd been in the Navy during World War II. Our first "home" was the first floor of a ramshackle old house in Tacoma, Washington, where Ray was finishing college and pastoring the young people in a church.

Right after our honeymoon, I began to feel seasick! Sherry was born ten months after the wedding, and that year I didn't learn very much about guiding a house. I was nauseated the whole nine months—morning, noon, and night. The day Sherry was born, I had lost my breakfast.

Ray is basically a tender lover, but no young husband is skilled yet at knowing how to handle a wife. His technique for dealing with my nausea was to try to talk me out of it: "It's all in your head." That just stirred up my anger. (One day he told me he'd read that pregnant women throw up because unconsciously they're trying to expel their babies—through their mouths. Right then I wanted to paste his nose all over his face.)

Then she arrived, this red-complected little mite with blond fuzz over her head. My mother came to care for us; boy, did she walk into a dirty house. By the time she left everything was shining, and I was determined to keep it that way. (It had always looked easy when the maid did it.)

Before I could find out, though, I was feeling that familiar queasiness in my stomach again—and when Sherry was eleven and a half months old, Margie was born. By this time we were living in the attic room of an old farmhouse in Pennsylvania (with bathroom "privileges" on the floor below), while Ray commuted an hour's drive away to Princeton Seminary in New Jersey.

When I could walk down the two flights of stairs to the old farmhouse living room, a friend came to call on the new baby and me. This made Sherry feel out of sorts, and she sat in her little rocking chair across the room, rocking and doing the two things she could do best: clicking her tongue and snapping her rubber panties. It's the last time I ever remember Sherry's being jealous of Margie. She has been a fabulous big sister, setting the tone for the other children to follow both spiritually and intellectually.

When Margie was two weeks old Sherry had her first birthday, and I sat on a tall kitchen stool to make her a chocolate cake. I still wasn't much of a cook, but Ray was a softie for anything chocolate—as he still is.

When Margie was five weeks old, we could finally move into a long-awaited student apartment on the Princeton campus. Up a winding stairwell to the third floor, and here was our own little nest—unfurnished! What fun. With our only savings we bought a love seat sofa bed for the living room, two maple cricket chairs, and a fibre rug. Daddy bought us a wonderful old upright piano! We slept on the sofa bed in the living room. In the one tiny bedroom the girls' two cribs just fit, along with a couple of secondhand chests of drawers. The kitchen could include a table, two chairs, and a high chair—and that was the apartment. I learned that I could nurse Margie and feed Sherry in her high chair all at once, and when they napped, I napped. My body was happy with those minimal assignments, so the house cleaning was minimal, too! One day I realized that the inside of the toilet was a dark-gray color, and it was comforting when, before long, Ray quietly cleaned it.

The summer that the girls were eighteen months and six months, we drove back in our clunky old car to Iowa to visit Ray's family. On the trip Sherry discovered cows in the fields, and Margie discovered the inside handles on the car door.

My little world was in our student apartment. It was there
Sherry was potty trained, with many an accident, and I learned
that it really isn't the *baby* who's trained, it's the *mother*. Every
hour on the hour, and if you forget—boy, there goes the old
fibre rug.

It was there Ray and I invented a recipe for ice cream (add
flavors so you don't taste the canned milk, freeze it in the ice
cube tray). It was cheap, and we dreamed of selling it around
for a profit, but we never had the time. Ray worked in the
library, he helped build houses, he gardened; and he went to
Tenafly on the train every entire weekend to be assistant pastor
in a church.

Still, he played football with the guys, and coaxed the babies
and me out of the apartment for picnics in the park and just
going for rides in the car.

Sherry was learning to talk! One day Margie was reaching up
to touch the piano keys, and Sherry, sitting on the couch, leaned
forward like a condescending little old grandmother and gave
Margie her first full sentence: "What dooning, Woggie? You
peena panno, h'mm?" We were astonished. We were sure we
were raising a genius. We made such a fuss over her that before
long Sherry was babbling words, words, words. And we had to
listen. To everything!

Margie was a drooler. For months I wiped her sweet little
chin and wiped her sweet little chin, and then I gave up and
kept her wearing bibs for years. Every bib got soaked and
changed like a diaper, and eventually, through endless launder-
ings, they got stiff and gray and could hold their own in a
gale-force wind. It was like wearing cement bibs; we marveled
at the power of spit. Later the doctor found she desperately
needed her adenoids out—tonsils, too—and Margie gave up her
career as a drooler.

The babies were sleepers. They were lively enough when
they were up, but they had long morning naps, long afternoon
naps, and went to bed at seven and slept until six in the morning. So I began to get out: I audited a class with Ray, typed his

term papers, played the organ for the seminary choir—and found I was pregnant again.

Yes, I cried. I stood in the middle of the living room with Ray holding me close, as I gave way and let it all out. *He* should have cried; he did all the laundry!

I took walks every day, with Sherry and Margie in the baby carriage, and I'd stop at the field to watch Ray playing football. Another mother was there with her little boy. I wondered to myself how you handle boys; I watched. This one was a husky, lively little fellow on his way to conquering the world—and he had a cold. Whenever the mother wanted to blow his nose, she just tackled him, put a knee on his chest, wiped, and let him up. *So that's how you handle boys,* I thought. . . .

There was no way three cribs would fit in our tiny bedroom. Princeton Seminary had not counted on people like us! But the largest student apartment on campus soon opened up, and it was really grand. Immediately my decorating instincts popped into bloom. This apartment was on the first floor and had a larger living room with French doors *and a balcony!* The kitchen had room for *two* tables (one to work on), two chairs, and three high chairs! And there were two tiny bedrooms: one could hold a borrowed double bed and two dressers; the other held all three cribs around the walls and two more dressers. How kind of the Lord!

When Sherry was twenty-eight months old and Margie seventeen months, we had a boy. A boy! Impossible! We had only girls. No, this one really was a boy. The nurses in the hospital tranquilized me all they dared, but I didn't sleep all night. Ray had his boy! Ray spread the news in our apartment building by punching each doorbell twice; once would have been for a girl.

Two daughters and a son! How rich we were. I could see how beautiful they would be. I was willing even to tackle a son and put my knee on his chest to wipe his nose.

A son!

"How many children have you?"

"Oh, we have three—two girls and a boy."

I could see them like flowers planted around a pretty dining table, sharing the day's events. I could see our son passing his sisters in height, and teasing them about it. All night long that September seventh I had visions of their future, and every one has come true, and far more. God gave me those promises, those visions; and I looked in His face and asked forgiveness for my tears and told Him I wanted to love Him more, be a better wife, a better mother, a better friend, a better woman.

37

Mother came and helped me slipcover the sofa bed. (Now we could sleep in a bedroom!) And we dyed sheets yellow and hung them for curtains, and painted the furniture. And there was room in the living room for other students to come in and sit down. I began to bake desserts and be ready with the coffeepot.

The sunlight streamed through the French door panes; I could see dust. I began to clean more. Chatting with the other wives, I learned how to get spots out of things, and we exchanged recipes. The little girls' hair was long enough for two perky ponytails apiece; they played out every day with a swarm of other students' kids. One time it dawned on me that I was responsible for eighty fingernails and toenails—including my own—but the Lord helped me stay on top most of the time.

One thing led to another: I painted a toy box for the children's room and put a gate across their door; when they played indoors in bad weather, that was to be their area. I kept the living room picked up, and kept the door open to the hallway for other students and wives to drop in.

By the next spring we found that the most "fun" kind of picnic was breakfast, when we could sit by the river and watch the Princeton University crews stroking. Ray was growing so "in grace and in knowledge" that we talked lots about what he was learning, and whether it was right or wrong, according to the Bible.

When we walked to the grocery store we put all three babies in the buggy! Ray insists people looked at him with a sort of "you beast!" stare, but I don't think so. They were just thinking how blond and handsome he was. God was good, and I was His Teacher's Pet.

Down I went that spring for major surgery. But Mother came again to keep three babies and comment on how the little apartment was cleaner. . . . Ray was so tender when he visited me in the hospital, and took time to play table games with me when I came home. . . . God was in His heaven, and all was right with the world.

The foreign missions board turned us down that spring because of my health, and Ray accepted a call to a Presbyterian church in a tiny hamlet in rural Pennsylvania.

June in Princeton was gorgeous. Ray was a dazzling blond wonder in his cap and gown. The babies were three, two, and almost one—three little chubby blond treasures. And Ray was ordained—a minister at last.

And starting the first Sunday in July, his sermons were knowledgeable, loving, and eloquent—at least according to his wife, who sat in the back pew with one little girl beside her, another asleep on her lap, and a baby boy dozing in the carriage next to the pew.

People ask me how our children survived being raised by a mother who writes books and goes speaking everywhere. My goodness, they were raised by a mother who . . .

· Nearly froze her fingers off hanging wet clothes in the backyard in the wintertime;

· Wasted dozens of tomatoes trying to learn to put up chutney;

· Scraped old wax off the kitchen floor to start fresh and discovered she was scraping off the floor, too;

· Changed diapers and spanked little ones and chirped over their funny, wonderful ways and anguished over their rebellions.

Even Nels, who came later in life, was mostly through grammar school before I wrote my first book or spoke at my first conference. God is wonderful about developing our gifts according to His own schedule for our lives. He knows which are the years when *there is no substitute for parenting.* It's the job that must be done then, not later.

It's when the cement is wet.

38

[M] MARGIE   [A] ANNE   [S] SHERRY

[M]   Hide the recorder in the plants . . . !

[A]   Oh, yes. . . . Okay, remember, you two, this has got to
be your deal, not mine; because I'm really just moderating this
thing so you won't giggle too much. I really want it to be your
ideas.

[S]   Let's start with grandparents. Um—I don't have very
many memories of Ortlund grandparents, but I have wonderful
memories of times at Sweet Acres [the country home in Pennsylvania for twenty-five years of Anne's parents, General Joe
and Betty Sweet].

[A]   The Ortlunds were just not very close geographically,
and then they died earlier.

[S]   Grandpa was your sweetie. He was the lover, he was a
tender person. My best memory of Grandpa is a little game we
would play. Particularly when others were around, we had a
sign language for "Do you love me?" He would reach over and
take my hand, and he would squeeze it four times, and that
would mean, "Do—you—love—me?"

And my response was three squeezes: "Yes—I—do."

136

To which he would squeeze twice: "How—much?"

And then I would squeeze just as hard as I possibly could, and that was how much. And that was a warm little thing between us that I remember as a kid.

[M]   And also, "I need a little something right here," pointing to his cheek.

[A]   He was a "lovey" grandparent; you were blessed to have him.

[S]   Tenderness and acceptance. I think we always felt from Grandpa that here was a nonjudgmental, understanding heart.

And Grandma, too, in her own way.

[M]   Very much so.

[S]   Yes. Now, Grandma wasn't as mushy—

[A]   No.

[S]   —as Grandpa, ever. But I remember going back to visit Grandpa and Grandma when I was eighteen. And Grandma had set up appointments for me to meet every friend they had in the world, and I remember her extreme pride in me. She was showing me off, and I knew it!

Grandmother, though, was significant in my life in the world of ideas. She loved to talk about significant things. I can remember—I was telling Margie earlier—standing in her kitchen, talking to her while she was fixing a meal, and she couldn't cook and talk at the same time, so cooking would go!

(Laughter.)

[A]   She was ideas. Father was relational.

[S]   My desires to be teaching the Word of God and that kind of thing—a lot of those desires come directly from Grandmother, as well as you, Mom.

[A]   Yes.

[S]   She was up at her kitchen table early in the morning, studying her Bible. I was very impressed with that as a kid: all the underlining in her Bible and the well-worn pages. And it wasn't that she'd had that Bible forever. She would get new ones periodically, but she just used her Bible all the time.

And I remember, that same trip when I was eighteen or so, her sitting down with me and going through the Scripture on the Second Coming, through section after section, and teaching me. And I madly took notes on everything, and I have them to this day.

[A]   That's a wonderful legacy. . . . I don't know if you two kids ever knew it, but through the years they had prayer every evening together, at bedtime, and Grandpa prayed for each grandchild by name—every night, year after year after year. Your name was always mentioned before the Lord once a day.

[M]   Oh, my.

[A]   As long as he had grandchildren, 'til he died. So that's a lot of prayers for you.

[M]   *Mm-hmm!*

[A]   Super! Grandparents. Now, what's next?

[M]   Let's talk about one basic message that we received as kids—over and over again, and that was, "I love you," and "You're important."

[S]   Yes!

[M]   And "You're unique." They all kind of flow in together. There seemed to be a concerted effort on the part of you and Daddy to create memories. In fact, it seems to me that all the way along, *doing* things was more important than getting things.

[A]   Experiences of togetherness have to come ahead of material things, don't they?

[M]   But that's unusual. Most people don't think that way.

[S]   They stay home on vacations to do some work.

[M]   —to save some money so they can paint the house or whatever. I always felt as though there was a real effort to create memories just like—well, I think of them as stones of remembrance—so that when we look back on them, we can talk about these and the effect they had on our lives and the good that they did.

[A]   You're our little nostalgia child, Margie.

[S]   Well, now, just a minute here! *(Giggles.)*

[M]   Sherry and I get to talking about these things, and we're a pile of mush by the end of the evening.

[S]   That is the truth!

[A]   Let's have a few more memories.

[M]   Big one: Cape Cod! [Our summer vacation spot, 1953–'58.]

[S]   Absolutely.

[A]   I think one of the important reasons why Cape Cod was so precious to all of us is simply because we were there as a whole family.

[M]   Yes. Right. Alone.

[A]   Nobody was doing anything else. Father wasn't working—

[S]   And part of it was that we took the same week and the same cabin every year, and it seemed like quite frequently we ended up going home on Buddy's birthday—

[M]   Uh-huh.

[S]   —so the celebration of Bud's birthday became part of the whole Cape Cod experience.

[A]   So it sounds like you're saying that when families can build a regularity into their life-style—if there can be a pattern —a time and place when fun happens—when the family celebrates—

[M]   You used to say something: every year at the end of vacation you'd say, "Only eleven more months to go!"

[S]   And Dad would always put some shells in the pocket of his bathing suit, to be left there all year long, until he got back to Cape Cod the next year and then start with new shells.

[M]   I think what is being said is that there was an independence of our family—not that it was separate from the body of Christ or the world in general—but what's—what's the word I want . . . ?

[S]   We were a *unit*. We had our own things that we did.

[A]   We built up our own vocabulary and expressions and traditions.

[M]   The memories, the identity, the feeling of belonging— I have a little picture in my mind when I see our family now, even though we're spread out, and we're doing different things —I still have a picture in my mind of the six of us Ortlunds, and also the children's spouses; and the picture I have is of all of us *marching.* And we have our arms locked, and we're marching, and we're very much together.

[A]   Praise the Lord.

Occasionally when we've marched, we've been out of step with each other! *(Laughter.)* Sherry, you were commenting on that before the tape turned on.

[S]   Well, there was one thing—forgive me, Mother—that I'm not going to do as a mother! When we were growing up, I remember becoming intrigued with rock music, and Mom and Dad not being real thrilled about this whole development; and one time you sat us down, you and Dad, and pulled out our records, which we'd bought with our own money, and you went through them, and what you didn't approve of was broken on the living-room floor.

[A]   We actually put them in a pile and stomped on them, remember?

[S]   Yes.

[A]   Oh, dear—!

[S]   And that's not a happy memory.

[A]   No.

[S]   And that's not something I would do. Nor do I believe you would do that at this point in your life.

[A]   We didn't do it with Nels. But you know, that's the problem: each generation is slightly "out of sync" with the next generation—you know?

[S]   Yes.

[A]   And it's hard to know what is worth blood and what is not. My mother would not let me listen to Kay Kayser or any of the old easy-swing things of the thirties and forties, and I think of that now as really pleasant stuff.

[S]   Yes.

[A]   I don't know; are there things you won't let your kids do that are cultural in the eighties, that maybe twenty years from now you'd think are not so bad?

[S]   No.

[A]   No? *(Laughter.)*

[A]   Drugs we can knock out for sure.

[M]   Yes.

[S]   For one thing, Walt and I have very strong feelings about movies and books—input into our kids' lives. But we also have very strong feelings about our own standards on those same issues as adults. In most cases, what we would not let our children see, we would also not go to see ourselves.

[M]   Yeah.

[A]   What do you say if you feel squeamish about something your kids want to do, and they say, "But *all* the kids are doing it! All the *church* kids are doing it"?

[M]   The standard line, the classic: "Tough beans." *(Laughter.)* We've already met that. And they cry and holler and kick and yell and fuss, but—that's the way it is.

[S]   I guess that's part of the feeling that we're not just run-of-the-mill—even the run-of-the-mill Christian world. We are a family, and we have our own set of standards. It really has nothing to do with anybody else's set of standards, or anybody else's life-style.

[A]   One thing I can remember telling you kids—not once but many times—is "Look, we've never been parents of teenagers before. Please hang loose with us; we don't know if we're doing it right or not. You have to do what we decide, but if you want to raise your teenagers differently someday, it'll probably be better!"

And you're so sweet, when you recall a bitter memory, I know you're not holding it against us now. In our zeal we did stupid things. And you forgive us, and we're still buddies.

[S]   Oh, yes!

[M]   Well, if we didn't allow our parents—and if our children don't allow us to be human and to overreact on occasion—then there's something terribly wrong. But I do remember you and Daddy being open to change.

[S]   Yes.

[M]   Vulnerable in many ways, willing to talk about it—not always, but sometimes—probably on the less crucial things.

And as I look back on the things you told me I couldn't do—I think of one thing in particular—it was going to a dance at school. I couldn't do that. Actually, you told me no, and I fussed, but I was inwardly sort of relieved, because I didn't know how to dance. I would have looked like a fool out there—and yet this way, I could say to this boy, "My parents won't let me go!" *(Laughter.)*—and blame it on you, and get off the hook!

[A]   We were the heavies!

[M]   Yes. And I think that happens to a lot of kids. Inwardly, they know they shouldn't do something; they know they don't *want* to do it; they know it would be compromising *their* values to do it—that the parents can be the heavies, and that's a legitimate role.

[A]   You bet.

[S]   Let's talk about something for a moment. Margie and I were talking recently about how you, Mother, are not the kind of woman who gets her thrills out of taking care of the home and kids. That's not been the thrill for you that it legitimately is for some women.

[A]   Mm-hmm.

[S]   And there have been times when that has been a hard pill for Margie and me to take, because we *wanted* to be the center of your life.

[A]   *(puzzled, amazed) Hmmm . . . !*

[S]   We have always loved you to death, and you were our model, and it would have been really nice at times to have just felt like you were just ready to drop everything for us.

[A]   *(unsure, groping around)* How long ago can you remember feeling that way?

[S]   Oh—last week. *(Laughter.)*

[A]   Oh, dear!

[S]   That is not an ending thing. I must admit there are times when I feel twinges.

But Margie and I were talking about how we as women find that we are, in our own attitudes toward life, very much like you. And neither of us really considers ourselves the kind of woman who more than anything else absolutely adores being a little homebody. Both of us have interests other than that, and, hopefully, we enjoy a broader perspective on life.

[A]   Isn't that interesting. What you're saying is, we're a combination of both grandparents. We are relational, but we are also absorbed by interests. You know?

[M]   Yes.

[A]   And we have to allow both in our lives.

[S]   But it's interesting that Margie and I give ourselves the break of not being totally child-centered; and yet because *we're* the child and you're the mother, that we want *you* to be totally child-centered. We were talking about how we have to allow you the same freedom to have other interests that we allow ourselves.

[A]   Isn't that interesting!

I must tell you, though, that one of the great thrills and satisfactions of my present life is the fact that you kids really genuinely love to be with us. We know that. We have fun just double-dating, or just palling around together. And that is one of the great joys that you will know when your kids are grown, and have their husbands and wives. When they just plain want to be with you for fun, that is the ultimate compliment.

[M]   If . . . if we're sharing hard memories, uh . . . here's another. I was gone back East on a vacation for six or eight weeks between high school and college, and in the intervening time you had taken my room, remember, and made it into the guest room—?

(Everybody guffaws uneasily.)

[M]   —because I was leaving!

[A]   Terrible!

[M]   Well, it's hard to grow up. It's hard to face those things. Do you remember, Mother, that I saw my room, and I just fell apart.

[A]   Oh-h-h—that was so insensitive of me to do that. I hadn't thought that—

[M]   —that it would affect me like that. Yes, well, I was so excited about going away to school, and everything seemed so wonderful, but still—it's hard to make that break. And that's wonderful, really.

[A]   A child who wants to go away to school and get independent—at the same time wants to have this secure place back home—right?—to come home to, that's unchanged.

[M]   Right. Yes, yes, definitely.

[A]   So it's good, as long as the parent can afford to, to keep the room intact, right?

[M]   Yes. I must say, though, that I knew, more and more as I grew older, that you and Daddy were together in yourselves, and there was a separation between you and us kids. And I liked that.

[S]   Yes.

[M]   You went away to a hotel in Los Angeles for your anniversaries, and I knew that was very romantic and special. I didn't know exactly what was going on *(Laughter)*—and I was very curious. *(More laughter.)*

[A]   And we weren't about to tell you!

[S]   And I was all caught up in books and wasn't curious at all! *(More hooting.)* I didn't have any idea!

[A]   Sherry looked up from her book, and there we were, back again! *(Laughter.)*

[M]   But I appreciated that, and I saw my friends' parents who were so tied to their children that I could tell they didn't have anything themselves, and I knew as I got closer to the time of leaving home that there was a good part in that. There was a sense of your kicking us out of the nest as well as our hopping out. And that's healthy.

[S]   I think I always sensed that we were being encouraged toward maturity, toward independence. And I look at that now as a very important part of child raising—to be always moving toward independence.

[A]   Sometimes did you feel insecure, that we were encouraging too much?

[M]   Of course!

[S]   Yes! The first year of our marriage, when we lived six blocks away from you and never saw you and you never called, I wondered what in the world was going on.

[A]   And *we* were scared to death that we would be interfering, and wanted to give you all this privacy, so the honeymooners could adjust.

[S]   Finally, when I understood, I've always appreciated that.

[A]   Well, again, we'd never had married kids before, and we were still learning how to do it: how much to involve yourself, and how much to hang back and stay away.

[S]   Even in adulthood there are times when you want more closeness and times when you want more individuality, and you just have to keep working at it and find out what's the appropriate response to each stage.

[A]   Yes.

[S]   Why don't we go on to attitudes toward life?

I guess I'll start out by saying that there was a general positiveness when we were growing up at home, that life was good, that life was fun, that being Christians was not a drudgery.

[M]   We had a strict household, but not a legalistic one.

[S]   And there was always this underlying thing, that it was terrific.

[M]   Yeah.

[A]   You know, you probably can't remember how many times you were dragged to church meetings, when we were in little churches without baby-sitters or nurseries; we couldn't afford baby-sitters, and the churches didn't have nurseries; and you've sat on more hard pews, through an awful lot of stuff, just because we wanted to expose you to the body of Christ. We knew that basically that's where the action was, and even though you were not getting anything out of it overtly, we wanted you to be absorbed into the ones we loved so much—God's people.

[S]   In that, all of us kids got the idea that the ministry is the best thing you could be involved in. The church is a good place to be.

I remember one of the boys in junior high giving me an awfully hard time about being a P.K. [preacher's kid]—that I should behave in a prim, proper fashion, and nobody else had to but I had to, because I was the P.K. That was a brand-new idea to me.

[A]   You were what, maybe thirteen or so?

[S]   *Mm-hmm.* Never before had that concept come across

from anybody—that I was supposed to be different.

We never sensed that; we were just people, and we were just doin' our thing—Jesus Christ's people, but it was not a burden laid on us—that we had to do something different.

[M]   I can remember when I was little—grade-school age—people would say to me, "What do you want to be when you grow up?" And very often I would respond, "A pastor's wife."

[A]   Oh, Margie, I remember that for years.

[M]   Yes! I watched my folks; they were busy; they were doing fun things; their life was involved with people; and I thought, "That's just got to be the most fun thing." Separate, even, from the spiritual issue, just as a way of life, it seemed grand.

[S]   When I think of Daddy, I think of fun.

[M]   Yeah!

[S]   He incorporated that same attitude into his churches. When we were kids, I remember East Glenville Church as being a very fun place. The atmosphere was fun.

[M]   Yes.

[S]   Now, when Daddy went to Lake Avenue Church, he decided he had to grow up. *(Giggles.)* [Ray was thirty-five when he accepted the call to Lake Avenue Church.] But I can remember there being a kind of banter back and forth between him and the East Glenville elders. And I remember potlucks at the church, where crazy skits were done.

[M]   Or here's another one: listening to parties going on downstairs, when we were upstairs in bed.

[S]   Yes! Dog and cat!

[M]   Dog and cat! *(Giggles.)* "Do you want to buy a dog?" "Does it bark?"

[A]   And do you remember once when the elders lugged an absolutely enormous rock into the middle of our living room in the middle of the night?

[M]   That's right!

[S]   And put a bottle of clam juice on the top of it to give us strength to get it out? *(Laughter.)*

I guess part of what Daddy's attitude was what we'd always been taught, to take Jesus Christ, and living for Jesus Christ, very seriously, but not to take ourselves too seriously; that life was meant to be fun; we just don't get overserious and introspective about ourselves.

Even as a family, we were not always conscious of being family. When we were at church, we were at church,—and we were doing things with other people.

I remember very strongly that we were taught to be others-centered. And as very small children, another person would come up to us, as frequently happens, saying, "How are you, little girl?" [*Giggle.*] You know!

[A]   *Mm-hmm.*

[S]   Little children don't know naturally to say, "I'm fine, thank you." That has to be taught. And we were taught that you looked the other person in the eye, faced him and talked to him directly.

[M]   I think, too, if the parents are actively *doing* ministry, if they're having people in their home, if their door is open. . . .

[S]   Yes—

[M]   —this will automatically be caught.

[S]   And we're trying to do that with our kids, too—to teach them to be very outward in their perspective, to be thinking of the needs of others, to be responding positively, aggressively, to others.

[A]   Let's mention their ages, just while we're sticking this on tape.

[S]   Mindy is eight and a half; Beth Anne is two and a half.

[M]   And Lisa is eleven and a half, and Laurie has just turned ten, and John (or Buddy) has just turned eight.

[A]   So they're all still wet cement, for sure, aren't they? And the things that you all are impressed with are even unconsciously impressing them.

[M]   Yes.

[S]   Can we just run through fun times?

[A]   Sure!

[S]   Battleship and Monopoly. We were a game-playing family.

[M]   Yes!

[S]   And it was very competitive. You didn't *let* anybody win. It was bloody! *(Laughter.)*

[M]   I'll never forget that time when we were at a football game (football is a big part of our memories), and Daddy, jumping up and down on the bleachers, and falling straight through.

[S]   Yes!

[A]   He had a lump on his hip for a year!

[M]   Exactly. That ties in with the whole attitude of an enthusiastic *yes* to life. I can remember him shadowboxing as he watched fights on TV.

[A]   Oh, he couldn't sit still! He still can't!

[M]   Because there's an involvement that he feels with everything in life. And you're not even a real athletic person, Mother, but you'd yell your lungs out at Blair High School games when Bud was playing football there. And there was a willingness to enter in and to be totally a part of the whole scene.

[S]   In fact, that's an important part of what we've been trying to establish in our family: that is, an attitude of never saying, "I don't feel like it."

[M]   Uh-huh. . . .

[S]   Everybody throws their suggestions out; we try a little bit of everything. You always try something.

[M]   "Say *yes!*"

[S]   Yes! "Let's try it!" Then if it isn't your favorite thing, you've discovered that it isn't your favorite thing, but you try it.

[A]   Don't you think there is a sense in which life is a piece of eternity, and when you subtract sin from it, there is still so much left—of fun and beauty and excitement and variety. And we really need to "go for it" in our interests, in our activities. You're right, Sherry; I want to do that more and more.

[S]   In fact, "if" we have our excesses—all three of us as adults (and I put the "if" in quotes because of course we do)— our excesses are an overenthusiasm, maybe, or that we are intense; we are all of us very focused, very aggressive.

[A]   *Mm-hmm.*

[M]   Do you remember, Sherry, John [then Margie's boyfriend, now her husband] and you and me driving home from Westmont [the girls' college]? I would arrive home in a heap, because John and Sherry would go to it, all the way—a two-and a half-hour drive.

[S]   Theology—

[M]   Philosophy—

[S]   Politics—

[M]   Whatever—

[S]   Everything! *(Laughter.)*

[M]   Each waiting for the other to finish a sentence.

[S]   Oh, no, not waiting! (Laughter.)

But it's interesting that all three of us have married people who are of that same intensity.

[M]   Yes.

[A]   Which makes the sparks fly—

[M]   Oh, yes.

[A]   —as it has with Ray and me. But we understand each other, and it's our desire to go hard after life and after God.

[S]   That's part of the whole idea of embracing everything, that you follow through something to its completion. You know: you go for it. If it's an argument, you follow that through to its completion. But every experience of life is gone through. You don't stop short of the full experience.

[A]   Well, each one of you is experiencing what Ray and I have been experiencing for thirty-four years—that really, a lot of garbage can happen when there is the underlying deep love and respect for each other.

[M]   *Mm-hmm.*

[A]   You can put up with a lot, you can forgive a lot, when you know basically you are committed to each other for life, and that's just the way it is.

[S, M]   *(in chorus)* Absolutely.

[M]   John and I told each other before we were married that the word *divorce* would never be used, even in a joking way, in our household, and it never has been, and it never will. That's not even an option at our very worst moments. There's an underlying commitment as long as we have this life.

[A]   I would say, too, that part of this spirit of "go for it" is that we will not even be satisfied with a bad marriage.

[M]   Yeah.

[A]   But there is something within us that says, "O dear Lord, I cannot live with this; I will not exist with this problem." As you were saying, Sherry, that we will see it through because we want a joyous—

[M]   —yes—

[A]   —loving marriage—

[S]   —yes—

[A]   —nothing less than that will do.

[S]   That's right.

[M]   I have been accused of having too great an influence on John, because people know that he bounces everything off me. There's a vital, basic togetherness that we have, and there's not a decision I don't think that's made in the church that we haven't talked through.

[S]   That's true with us. Walt has told me everything about his work; there's been this constant flow of talk all the way along. I've always been a participant in his life, and he in mine.

[A]   Now, do you two suppose that that's affected your children directly or indirectly?

[S]   *(Giggles)* Well, Mindy talks all the time!

[M]   Where does she get that? I think I've got five minutes on this tape so far. Sherry's got the other ninety-five!
(Laughter.)

[A]   So it's not a case of Mindy's growing up quiet because she never got a word in edgewise?

[S]   No! No, no, no.

[A]   Okay.

[M]   We draw our children out. For instance, every Sunday noon we go out to eat, just as we did when *we* were growing up, and that's our time to talk. And nobody goes with us; and we don't just talk, the two of us, but we draw the children out.

[S]   We have family night.

[M]   We have family night, too.

[S]   And not always but sometimes, Mindy gets to choose

anything within a certain budget, and we do it. Sometimes it's with Beth Anne, sometimes without her. But Mindy looks forward to that. She knows the focus is going to be on her, and on us, as a family, and we aren't going to talk shop, we aren't going to talk church, we're just going to have fun.

Sometimes it's popcorn and games at home, when the budget's slim; sometimes it's going miniature golfing, or a Disney movie.

[A]   Do you remember the years that Father got so pressured with every-evening meetings that breakfasts were our big thing?

[M]   Yes. Right.

[A]   Our real family time each day was breakfast.

[S]   And you cooked special. Fish! For breakfast!

[A]   Certainly!

[S]   Goldenrod eggs. . . .

[M]   They were wonderful. You could really cook good breakfasts.

[A]   And toasted bacon sandwiches.

[M]   Oh! Yummy!

[A]   And when we had fish, sometimes broiled tomato halves.

[M]   And you made the most wonderful cinnamon toast.

[A]   And fried scrapple—or fried Cream of Wheat, or mush, with syrup.

[M]   Oh, yummy.

[S]   Now, I want to add that—no. *(Giggles.)*

[M]   I loved it all!

[A]   I'm getting defensive, because Sherry always talks about my bad cooking.

[M]   You're a fantastic cook!

[S]   Listen, I have to say there's *something* you can't do! It makes me feel better.

[A]   Oh, dear. . . .

What have we left uncovered, from these notes of yours?

[S]   I want to add that as adults we are still creating family memories. I think that's significant.

[A]   You mean within the Ortlund family?

[S]   Yes. That our relationship did not end with adulthood. The whole Christmas Eve family tradition—getting together and dragging out the old slides and movies; it's fun to have your spouses join in and be part of the creation of family memories. John was the one who brought up the old picture of Mom— *(Screams of laughter.)*

[M]   —and slipped in the slide every other picture.

[S]   The hairdos were terrible in those days. It was all skinned close to your head. And Mother had this little flat hat that perched on top, and in this picture she was laughing and her mouth was wide open, and it was UG-LEE! [*Howls of laughter, finally subsiding.*]

[A]   You know, I must say, and this is not just to be Pollyanna or anything, but for the record—it was years and years ago that you girls began first helping me learn to put on makeup, and you were with it and I was not. [*Giggles.*] And you always felt free to say, "Mother, that outfit is really out of it," and "Please shape up." I have learned so much from you. I am so grateful that as you've become adults, and even before, you have taught me so much, and I need so much to learn from you. And as you grew, and grew out from under my influence, God was putting wonderful influences around you that I needed. And you have really felt free in our security with each other to keep teaching me, so that we are now three women learning from each other. And I have gotten so many good things out of life that you have taught me, and I'm grateful, and I say *thank you,* and keep it up. *(Murmurs of response.)*

Well, anything else on the waterfront that we need to cover? [*Silence.*]

You both have been tremendous.

[S]   Well, Nels offered a page, and this is typical of us verbal girls. [*Giggles.*]

[A]   One tape wouldn't even do it! But I'm thankful we didn't tape over the Elvis Presley tape, Margie! *(Laughter.)*

[A]   Is that it?

[M]   That's it.

39

(Incidentally, Bud is the daddy of Eric, four; Krista, three; and Dane, one. They hang all over him when he's home. He and Jani are like a couple of ballet dancers, balancing jobs. One puts on socks, the other, shoes. . . .

"Daddy," said Eric when Ray and I were last visiting them, "are we going to build a fire and read *Winnie the Pooh* tonight?" They *always* build a fire and read *Winnie the Pooh,* and I think Eric was afraid the schedule might be upset because grandparents were visiting.

They built a fire and read *Winnie the Pooh.*)

I am thankful for the privilege of participating in this written ministry.

A concept which means a great deal to me as a father is what Dr. Hudson Armerding calls in his book *Leadership,* our "minority status." As Bible-believing Christians (or, at least we want to be such), we are sojourners through a foreign land. Our identity, perspective, aims and destiny are unique among our fellow men in so far as these great realities are not earthbound or of human origination. We are a new creation in Christ amid a dead world. Furthermore, that dead world comprises the majority viewpoint in society and is dominated by "the god of this world." My point is that we Christians, we parents and children, must become rebels in our minds. By a deliberate, theologically founded choice, we are to live as iconoclasts while we remain resident in Satan's kingdom, challenging the validity of the assumptions, values and morals controlling men's minds in our age. We must not dishonor our Lord through complicity with the world system which has rejected Him.

I am reminded, for example, of Samson's demand for a Philistine woman to be his wife (Judges 14). In their spineless reply his parents whimpered, "Isn't there some nice Israelite girl you could choose? Must you go to the uncircumcised Philistines for a wife?" They should have said something like, "Son, such an act would be against God [Deuteronomy 7:3]. The unique purposes He has for us in this world require that we marry within Israel. Our Lord has spoken. If you intend to serve Him, you know what you should do." We cannot force our children to follow God rather than the world, but we can try to put forth the issues as clearly as possible lest our kids fail to see the radical choice before them. As Scripture says, "Anyone who chooses to be a friend of the world becomes an enemy of God" (James 4:4).

Certainly, we want to seek our Lord's grace to be delivered from a threatened "fortress mentality," from any cynical view of life in general, or from a spirit of self-righteous religious superiority as we survey the world. Too, we parents must not easily assume that we ourselves are not significantly influenced by the world's perspective, for we are. And neither do we want to take a firm stand on an issue which our Lord does not view as important. How we need wisdom and discernment! And our Lord has that needed wisdom revealed in Scripture. We also have His promise to complete the good work begun in us Christian parents and children. May it be in our hearts who have such a hope to teach and persuade our children to think for themselves, to be faithful to their Lord, and not compromise their Christian integrity in the face of the majority opinion.

40

Fifteen-year-old Nels started into tenth grade this fall at the Stony Brook School on Long Island, New York. It's great for him, but tough. Lots of love, hard studies, coats and ties at dinner every night—and they do their own laundry.

Brother! I hope his clothes come out all right. I thought of Nels, as I read about a college freshman shopping for his school clothes. He asked an equally young clerk what SHRINK RESIS-TANT meant on the shirt he was looking at.

The clerk hesitated, then took a stab at it: "I think it means the shirt does shrink, but it doesn't want to."

Anyway, Nels wrote his contribution, absolutely unaided by me, on the plane going to school.

When I was ten years old I played little league baseball. I was thought of as a sissy because I went to church and my dad was a preacher. Mom and dad had warned me about this so I wasn't bothered one day when one of my friends who apparently was trying to change that, called me a "Jesus freak." If it weren't for my parents, I would have hit the bad time blues by now. Mom and Dad have taught me and my brother and sisters not to be antagonized by people who can't accept the fact that a christian is human, too, and therefore must treat us badly. My parents have "cemented" me into their ways and beleifs. I don't always agree with them, but I don't think we would have a normal family if everything was perfect. When it comes right down to it, I will always be 100% behind my folks and I'm sure my brother and sisters would agree with me.

My parents have never pressured me to follow in their footsteps or anything of the sort, although I would be proud to do what they are doing now. In the past, and now, as I sit on the plane to my new school, I have admired what they do.

As I sit here I think of some of the things where certain impressions of them can be seen in me or my brother and sisters. For instance, my mom's strong will, a good thing to have of course, is seen in all of us kids. And when our wills clash, Bang!!!

Or my dad's way of laughing, listening, or talking, which each of us has picked up just from being around him. Impressions of all kinds can be picked up from your parents in just the few years you are with your folks.

I think of the way a child is brought up as a tree with roots but no branches. Growing still, but your parents let you grow your own branches in life after they've helped grow your roots.

I love my folks and always will, but really I have no choice because part of me is them and I like myself so that automatically says I like them too.

The End

Section IV

About You and All of Us ...

41

I'm praying that this section is the blockbuster. I've been anticipating writing it for so long! This is the good news that *nobody's cement needs to have hardened.*

"What?" you say. "You don't know me. It's not that I like it, but I see how set I've become in what I think about morals and politics and religion and government and anything you want to name. And my habits are so set; I've done things the same dumb way for so long.

"It's too late to change me. I'm 'sot in my ways.' And it's too late for our family to change. Our habits are too fixed."

Why did you just say, "It's not that I like it"? Because *God has built hope into you—that your future will be better than your present, that you can still become what you long to be.*

And why does He build this hope into you? Because He wants you to discover how strong His big hands are, to change you, and to change your family. Then He'll get all the glory!

Modern secular thinking is the opposite. It tells you that you're the product of the way your mother buttoned you up, and how she neglected to wipe your nose—and that's just the way you are. They would indicate that you can be analyzed to understand yourself better, but you can't change.

That's Satan's lie. He spreads around that story because he wants to keep all his people fixed in position, thinking they can't get out.

When you were a kid did you play the game Freeze,—running like crazy, until the one who was "it" suddenly yelled the word, and then you were locked into position? Satan is busy shouting "Freeze!"—doing his best to get people to stay their ugly old selves, discouraged from thinking that they could ever be different.

"It's the way you were raised as a child," says Satan. "You're 'in cement.' "

Paul Tournier admits the problem. He says in *The Strong and the Weak,*

> It is as difficult to help a strong man to see his weakness as it is to assist a weak man to regain confidence. . . .

But he goes right on to say that God's grace will do it:

> Since we are at one and the same time both strong and weak, grace also at one and the same time convinces of wretchedness and saves us from despair—it breaks and restores us.

The grace of God! The love of God! The favor of God, unearned and undeserved—that's the enormous miracle power that can change and remake and remold your cement. Jeremiah said it this way:

> I went down to the potter's house, and I saw him working at the wheel. But the pot he was shaping from the clay was marred in his hands; so the potter *formed it into another pot,* shaping it *as seemed best to him.*
>
> Then the word of the Lord came to me: ". . . can I not do with you as this potter does? . . . Like clay in the hand of the potter, *so are you in my hand. . . .*
>
> Jeremiah 18:3–6 (italics mine)

The loving, gracious hands of God are strong enough to re-work any life on this earth. Even yours.

Augustine, in early Church history, was reshaped by God after having a well-deserved reputation of sleeping around with the girls. One day as he was walking down a street, one of his old girl friends spotted him.

"Augustine!" she called.

Augustine didn't answer; he just quickened his pace.

"Augustine," she called again, "it is I!"

Augustine began to run—as he called back to her, "But I am not I!"

Augustine's clay, the original material, was the same, but God had reworked him into a completely different shape, a new pot.

42

I had a phone call recently.

"Anne," said an unfamiliar voice, "this is Connie Gonzales. Do you remember me?"

I thought. "Honestly, I don't," I said. "Help me."

"Twelve years ago I phoned you. I was a young heavy-set Mexican girl who'd just been caught stealing over ten thousand dollars from my boss at work. I asked you if I could talk to you."

"Really?" I said, mentally fumbling around.

"I remember it was dinnertime, and my need was really urgent, and you left your family and didn't eat any dinner and met me at your church to talk to me."

"Connie," I said, "I've really forgotten."

"Well, I told you that stealing was a pattern with me, and that I'd been doing it for years, and that they were just about to catch up with me, and I'd go on trial for grand larceny, and I asked you if I should turn myself in."

A vague memory began to stir in my mind. "And I encouraged you to turn yourself in, didn't I?"

"You went with me to the police station, and I did—but first you led me to accept Jesus Christ."

"Connie, it's coming back to me. It's been so long. How are you doing?" I asked.

"I read your book *Disciplines of the Beautiful Woman* recently," she said, "and I was telling my girl friend that I knew

you and that you led me to Christ, and she thought I should call
you and encourage you."

"Tell me about yourself," I said.

"I went to a California women's prison," said Connie, "and it
was rough, but I always knew God loved me. I never had anybody love me before, and I knew He really did, and that He was
helping me every day.

"After a while I got paroled on good behavior, and I started
in to work. And there was a scientist in our office, David, and
he fell in love with me, and I was really scared to tell him about
my background. But I knew he was a good Christian, and he
worked hard in his church and everything, so I really told him
the whole story.

"And do you know, Anne, he just said to me, 'My, Connie, you
must have really been hurting from a lack of love to do that. I
would like to make it up to you and love you for all the rest of
your life.'

"Anne," said Connie, "I'm married to my wonderful husband, David, and we have two darling little boys. You wouldn't
know me—I've slimmed way down; and we're both active in
our church. . . . It's so wonderful. . . . We have so many friends
who love the Lord. . . . I almost never tell my background—just
once in a while, when I can really help somebody who's hurting,
then I tell it.

"But my name is Connie Taylor now; and Anne, we live in a
beautiful big house. Listen, I have more room in our master
bedroom than I had in my whole little shack when I was stealing
from other people.

"Anne, I just had to encourage you. Thank you for telling me
that God loves me. I say it over and over, and I read it in the
Bible, and I hear our pastor say it, and I know that He really
does love me.

"And David loves me, too, and he says it over and over and
over.

"I hear those two things all the time, God loves me and David
loves me. And they've changed my whole life."

43

We had lunch this noon with our dear friends Phil and Audrey. Phil was in a mood to talk, and he told us what a dumb, stumbling, rebellious child he'd been.

"My folks said I couldn't do anything," said Phil, "so I didn't! My father was a machinist—so clever with his hands—and my mother was mechanical, too. But they always said I was the dumb one.

"I was in junior-high school when I tried to build our dog a little house. I'd never built anything in my life! And I can remember my father grabbing the saw out of my hand and saying, 'Here, let me do that. You won't get it straight down the middle.'

"Something rose up inside of me," said Phil. "I was so angry and so frustrated, I said to myself, *I'll never touch a saw again. I'll never try to make anything as long as I live. I'm through! I've had it!*"

Phil described to us his high-school years. "It took me five years to get through. I flunked lots of courses. I didn't know how to study; I couldn't concentrate; I didn't care. My folks had programmed me: they said I was dumb and bad, so that was just what I was!"

But God was higher and stronger than all that. God's plans for Phil were going on anyway, and new forces began to come into effect. He actually met the Lord in the Army, and was exposed to other young men who were serious about their Christian walk.

Then Phil married Audrey, and Audrey believed in him. Several babies later, Audrey encouraged Phil to apply at a really good college! Phil was tested; he was intelligent enough. He took extra courses to qualify to enter.

He struggled through years of college—but he was turning around. A major breakthrough came when Audrey was pregnant with their fourth baby, and a man said he'd build them a house cheap. He'd barely laid the foundation when he walked off the job. . . .

Phil built his house.

Today, with his master's degree, he's done well for years as a personnel specialist. His four children are outstanding, and so are Phil and Audrey.

You should have seen him sparkle at lunch as he told about his latest achievements.

"I fixed my car totally myself," he said. "And now I'm working on an oil painting—mountains and a stream—. . . . It's really turning out good!"

Audrey sat by quietly listening, with happy eyes.

44

Oh, if I could tell you how true this is in my own life! I am absolutely unafraid of the damage done to little Betty Ann Sweet. The Red Hands pursuing, the garbage can threats—it's true that they made cement prints inside of me. And many people live their lives only as the sum total of all the imprints made upon them when they were young and impressionable.

Those people are the ones who refuse to be worked on and remade by God's powerful, reshaping grace.

I didn't tell you the best part of the story; I saved it for the last. I'm a new person! And so can you be a new person.

Even little Betty Ann Sweet's name got changed. Mother dropped the "Betty," and I put an *E* on "Ann." And then I lost the name "Sweet" when I married Ray Ortlund.

(When I was engaged to Ray, I thought, "At last! I won't hear any more quips about my name. No more puns!" And the first thing Ray began to call me was "Little Ortlund Annie"!)

How did I get changed? I accepted Jesus Christ into my heart and life, to be my Savior from all my sins and fears, and to rework me into whatever shape He desired.

And all by Himself, He implanted into me a reciprocal love for Himself. Anne Ortlund loves the Lord! That's the strongest, most driving force of my life. I know it. It powerfully shapes, controls, and motivates the little Betty Ann inside of me. It works—no, not *it* but *He*—works constantly seeking to win over

my basic tendencies to hide, to sleep too long, to show off, to be
hasty, to lie, to procrastinate, to be dull, to hang back. . . . And
a thousand more of Betty Ann's characteristics.

When I say to Ray, "I'm basically mousy," he laughs. I know
it's true, remembering my imprints, but he only gets occasional
hints of Betty Ann. (Earlier this year, the way a child reverts to
thumb sucking, I surprised him with a month-long regression
into insecurity.)

But the Holy Spirit lures me on, making me pursue Him
more, love harder, laugh more, work longer. He makes me
impatient with meaninglessness, with waste, with vulgarity.
Satan's empire is Dullsville to me!

I love to live in eternity. The caverns of conceiving and pursuing and achieving are arched so high over my head that I am
lost below. Yet I have a conviction that I will expand to inhabit
them all before I'm done. I'll fly! I'll soar! God is so vast, and God
is drawing me on. God is so vast,—but He loves me, and He's
laughing as He tugs at me.

Betty Ann Sweet is fading more and more. My sin has been
dealt with, forgiven, and forgotten. Not often do I wring those
little hands; I reach them up to Him, and to *up*. Whatever the
future is, for me it is up.

45

Let me suggest a twofold plan of attack for you.

Number one: see yourself *as God sees you:* a little child of
eternity, moldable and pliable.
Number two: surrender yourself totally under His hands.
Confess your faults, your sins—and let God powerfully rework
your life, and the life of your family.

First, see yourself through God's eyes.

The proud, the "adults" of this world, the people who think
they have it all together—or can get it all together—by their
own efforts, God resists. He works against them. He makes them
stumble. He puts holes in their pockets. He hassles them. He
opposes them.

The Old and New Testaments say it together in chorus: "He
mocks proud mockers *but gives grace to the humble"* (Proverbs
3:34; *see also* James 4:6, italics mine.)

A little child is humble. He's not hardened yet—not sophisticated; he's impressionable; he's moldable.

We ate dinner recently with our friends the Tuckers. Little
Brian didn't care about seeing the menu. He just kept banging
on his daddy's arm and saying, "Daddy, tell me what I want!"

Yes, a little child is pliable and shapable. Jesus said, "I tell you
the truth, unless you change and become like little children,

you will never enter the kingdom of heaven." And He pulled
a little one next to Him right then, and He said, "Therefore,
whoever humbles himself like this child is the greatest in the
kingdom of heaven" (Matthew 18:3, 4).

Tell me what I want. Beautiful. May the Lord make us all in
our hearts like little Brian: "Heavenly Father, *tell me what I
want.*"

God calls His own His children, and that's what He wants us
to be: not childish, but childlike! The values of being childlike
are immense: you'll be forever teachable, dependent, and trust-
ing—uncorrupted and uncynical. You won't "crust over" and
harden, so you can be always growing and discovering and
changing and improving.

Childlike people God will watch over: "The Lord protects the
simplehearted . . ." says Psalms 116:6.

One of the deep books of the *Old* Testament is Proverbs, a
"family" book written to all of us—and addressed to MY SON. If
we'll humbly assume that posture, then we're in a position to
learn all that wisdom.

One of the deep books of the *New* Testament is First John,
a "family" book written to all of us, and addressed to "my little
children." That's a tender term: literally, "my little born ones,"
or as the Scottish say, "my bairns." And we have to be one of
His bairns to absorb the depths of First John.

Why do troubles come to you? Proverbs 3:11, 12 tells you
why:

> My son, do not despise the Lord's discipline and do not
> resent his rebuke, because the Lord disciplines those he
> loves, as a father the son he delights in.

The New Testament quotes these verses and goes on to say,

> Endure hardship as discipline; God is treating you as
> sons. For what son is not disciplined by his father? If you
> are not disciplined (and everyone undergoes discipline),
> then you are illegitimate children and not true sons. . . .

No discipline seems pleasant at the time, but painful.
Later on, however, it produces a harvest of righteousness
and peace for those who have been trained by it.

Hebrews 12:7, 8, 11

This is significant. Notice it carefully. How can you train the children in your life if you refuse to be trained?

How can you teach them to obey you, if you will not obey God? *This is the key to your children's obedience.*

You tell your child, "Go to bed." Does he move quickly? God is telling you, "Go—to prayer meeting, your unsaved neighbor, the mission field, a friend who's disagreeing with you. . . ." Are you moving quickly to obey Him?

You tell your child, "Eat your food." Are you obeying your heavenly Parent when He says, "Feed on My Word"?

You give your child an allowance, and part of your training is to guide him as he spends it. God gives you an allowance of money, too. Do you let Him guide you in spending it?

Deuteronomy 8:5 says, "Know then in your heart that as a man disciplines his son, so the Lord your God disciplines you."

Whatever God is telling you to do, do it. Humble yourself as a little child to Him. If you obey, your children will also learn to.

You see the plan: God is our perfect Model, our heavenly Parent, and the Source of all parenting. We're to follow Him around, watch Him, copy Him, love Him—just like happy kids around their daddy; and from Him we'll get the pattern to repeat in parenting our own.

"Be imitators of God, therefore, as dearly loved children . . ." (Ephesians 5:1). And when you do, you can *expect to be like Him*—just as your kids turn out to be like you!

The key to your child is you. When Samson's parents were told by an angel, before he was ever conceived, that they would have a son, their first question was your natural question: "Teach us how to bring up the boy who is to be born" (*see* Judges 13).

Do you know, the angel gave no rules on child training. He only talked about the personal living of the parents!

There's no cut-and-dried formula for child raising, and that's why the Bible doesn't give any. Heavens! Did you ever think: biblical parents, following God's orders, have been known to hide their babies in baskets in a river, shunt them off to battle with food and let them actually get involved in the fighting, and even take them up on a mountain to kill them? In each case, the result was the shaping of one of the world's great leaders.

Are there children around you depending on your modeling and training? Then closely follow the Lord. *Just follow Him.* He will not always lead you the way He leads someone else. But follow Him as His teachable, humble child, and two things will happen.

First, you will grow strong and spiritually mature.

And second: the children around you will become teachable and humble, and so they, too, will grow strong and spiritually mature!

46

Think of yourself, my friend, as a child of eternity. If the little ones around you are tomorrow's world, in a vaster, far more exciting sense you are eternity's world. *You are part of the future population on the other side.*

Are you getting shaped and trained for it? The Bible is full of descriptions of rewards for those who got ready. Yes, and apparently there is a hierarchy there; Jesus talked a lot about being "greatest in the kingdom" and "least in the kingdom."

Oh, what a solemn thought! I sit here writing to you and praying, "Spirit of the living God, fall afresh on me! Mold me, make me, fill me, use me. . . ."

The prerequisite for ever arriving there is being born into His family in the first place. Don't miss that! John 1:12, 13 says that to all who receive Jesus Christ, who believe on His name, He gives "the right to become the children of God—children born not of natural descent, nor of human decision or a husband's will, but born of God."

And Jesus says, "I tell you the truth, unless a man is born again, he cannot see the kingdom of God" (John 3:3). This is a permanent miracle-birth, when you are born again "not of perishable seed [or semen], but of imperishable, through the living and enduring word of God" (1 Peter 1:23).

Don't think for a minute that everybody's just naturally a child of God and headed for heaven. Jesus was one day confronting men with hard, rebellious hearts.

" 'You are doing the things your own father does.'

" 'We are not illegitimate children,' they protested. 'The only Father we have is God himself.'

"Jesus said to them, 'If God were your Father, you would love me, for I came from God and now am here. I have not come on my own; but he sent me. Why is my language not clear to you? Because you are unable to hear what I say. You belong to your father, the devil . . .' " (John 8:41–44).

So, my friend yet spiritually unborn, as you read this, God's Spirit is pleading with you to do the first thing you need to do: surrender yourself to Him for His initial work of salvation in your life. If you don't think you need it, God can't do anything for you. But if you'll humble yourself and admit your need, He will respond with His total forgiveness, cleansing, and fresh start for eternity.

He's willing to do it in this very moment.

47

As you read this, if you know that you are already God's child, surrender yourself now and continually to stay malleable in His hands. Not to unbelievers but to "holy brothers who share in the heavenly calling" the writer to the Book of Hebrews pled three times, "Today, if you hear His voice, *do not harden your hearts*" (*see* 3:7, 15; 14:7). God leaves us with our free wills intact. In our spirits we can get old, dull, stale, immovable. Any age can get that way. I've known Christian young people who were fearful, conservative, unwilling to bend or risk or adventure.

We *can* harden—but we never need to. The Master Potter says that we are His workmanship (Ephesians 2:10), and He wants us to stay pliable under His hands as He conforms us all to the image of His Son (*see* Romans 8:29). Praise the Lord. He is stronger than we are, and Philippians 1:6 promises that He will eventually get us to perfection, because that's His gracious plan.

But how we can rebel and resist Him and grieve His Spirit in the process! If you do, my friend, you will probably also produce rebellious, resistant children.

There was a couple in their midthirties in an earlier church that Ray pastored who were hardening fast. They seemed to make it their business to resist both God and Ray! They were debaters and objectors over any issue in congregational meetings; every pastor knows their kind.

One day their junior-high-age son was tramping on some new baby grass just planted at the church, and Ray said, "Hey, my friend, how about staying on the sidewalk till the grass grows?"

"I don't have to," he said. "My parents say you're anti-intellectual."

Out of the mouths of thirteen-year-olds! Ray mourned to me about it, "Resistance breeds resistance." And that young boy, very gifted mentally, grew up to damage his brain with hard drugs and today has no contact with anybody, not even his parents.

Surrender yourself totally to God's good work upon you. If you're humble and willing, His power will "unharden" your hardening! He can reverse the process. He can stir the hardening cement and reshape before it finally sets. He can start with you afresh. God is the God of new beginnings.

As long as you're alive, you can soften and begin again under His hands. But when eternity comes—*suddenly,* in an instant —you will be permanently hardened cement. The Bible ends with these words about the Final Day:

> Let him who does wrong continue to do wrong; let him who is vile continue to be vile; let him who does right continue to do right; and let him who is holy continue to be holy.

> Revelation 22:11

At that point everyone will at last be permanently fixed. You've seen it pictured on television: people are moving and talking—and suddenly the scene is frozen into a still shot. . . .

And only God knows when His "instant" will be.

48

But are you feeling "fixed" right now? Reworking is a deeply powerful thing. You've been so long the way you are; maybe you've almost lost hope.

Paul Tournier writes,

It is not easy to break free from our psychological reactions. The first requisite, of course, is to recognize them. But that is not enough. Their determinism is powerful. It is nourished . . . by the knowledge we have of our inner weaknesses.

That is why true liberty is not to be found without the confession of our sins. And the experience leads at once to dedication, to a decision in every circumstance to choose God's will.

The Strong and the Weak

The confession of our sins! He says it in five words, and we almost lose in their brevity the crashing power of the experience, the agony of it, the embarrassment.

I had a habit I just couldn't tell *anybody.* I wrestled with it; I struggled; I made good resolutions; I relapsed; I made more resolutions; I failed.

Finally I knew what I had to do. I had to tell Ray. *Tell*

Ray—? I'd die first. A few more months of fresh resolutions and more relapses. . . .

Buried in his arms, I told him. It wasn't nearly as hard on him as it was on me. And that was that: it was over. The confession was over,—and better yet, so was the habit. And that was a quarter of a century ago! God is so wonderful.

Says Sally Folger Dye,

> Facing the truth is the only way to break out from behind the . . . mask [of hypocrisy]. It seems that one has to acknowledge falling short, accept cleansing for unacceptable emotions and actions, and appropriate the real [acceptance] provided by God's grace, realizing that God loves, forgives, and accepts everyone who comes to Him with a humble heart.

We saw that the lift-up technique with a teenager means getting lower in order to help him grow upward. And amazingly, the lift-up technique with yourself means getting lower, too—in order to help yourself grow upward. The wonders of the methods of God!

The way to up is down.

49

To whom must you apologize?

It's just like those affirmations: first to God, then to each other. That's the way new beginnings begin.

Will you get on your knees? Will you get on your face before Him? The messes we have made with our families, with our relationships, have offended Him. Will you tell Him so?

Become as a little child. Confess to Him that you're weak, you're foolish, you're penniless, you're unlearned, you're unskilled, you're uncouth—you're everything a child is.

Confess to Him your absolute and final inadequacy in yourself.

If you want to begin to experience His lifting and renewal, it's the only way. The way to up is down!

> For this is what the high and lofty One says—
> he who lives forever, whose name is holy:
> "I live in a high and holy place,
> but also with him who is contrite and lowly in spirit,
> to revive the spirit of the lowly
> and to revive the heart of the contrite.

Isaiah 57:15

The sacrifices of God are a broken spirit;
   a broken and contrite heart,
   O God, you will not despise.

                                             Psalms 51:17

Expose to Him all your deficiencies. Jesus loved the man who
prayed, "Lord, be merciful to me, a sinner."
   I say it, too, as I write these words.

   Repent, then, and turn to God, so that your sins may
be wiped out, that times of refreshing may come from
the Lord.

                                             Acts 3:19

50

The "last days" are rushing upon us. God predicted how they would be—that the children would be disobedient to parents (2 Timothy 3:2)—eventually to the point of totally rebelling against them and having them put to death! (Matthew 10:21).

We're on the way. Families are falling apart. Divorce is a raging river. "Single adults" are multiplying—and so are sexual sins. More and more children are raised in confusion, and they're growing up to make second-generation messes. And in the rare homes still intact with both parents, there's often tension and yelling and noncommunication and too fast a pace.

Malachi said that either the hearts of the fathers must once again be turned toward the children, and the hearts of the children turned to their fathers—"or else [God] will come and strike the land with a curse" (Malachi 4:6).

The relationships between the generations must be healed, or else God's patience with us will run out.

Are your parents still living? Apologize to them for all your orneriness as a child (maybe even as a grown child. I was forty-six before I did that—and oh, it created such a warm, loving time for us!) If they're at a distance, phone, or at least write a letter. But hugs are best!

And right now, if you're a parent, turn your heart toward your children. If they're grown and away from you, they need an apology, by phone or letter. Knit your hearts closely, closely together.

And if they're still at home and old enough to understand, they need apologies, too. You need a fresh start with them. Asking for forgiveness begins the process of breaking up the hardening mold of wrong habit patterns and negative thoughts toward each other.

What needs to be confessed?

· You've been preoccupied, and slighted them when they needed attention. . . .

· You moved too often on your job, and that was upsetting to them. . . .

· You haven't always faced them with their sins (confrontations are hard for you); you didn't always punish them when they needed you to, and their bad habits remain as a testimony against you. . . .

· You sinned by omission—withholding from them Bible study and prayer. . . .

· You've been tired sometimes, and you've yelled at them; you've been overharsh and injured them. . . .

· You've unthinkingly withheld the support of affirmations, and injured them. . . .

· You've blown it. . . .

Tell them.

Tell them how sorry you are. And ask their forgiveness.

51

Only a few months ago Ray and I made a date with Nels and drove out into the hills overlooking Newport Beach.

"Nels," said Ray, "I've goofed a lot as a dad. I love you very much, but I've said and done a lot of dumb things through your fifteen years. I know I've hurt and not helped lots of times, and I just want you to know that I'm sorry."

There was a long silence. Nels didn't quite know how to respond.

"Are you leading up to something?" he asked.

"Not a thing," said Ray. "I just wanted to say that for all the times I've blundered and hurt you and done or said stupid things to you, to put you down or make life tougher for you, I really am sorry. I just wanted to apologize."

I chimed in from the backseat of the car. "Nels, we didn't do dumb things on purpose; but we know we've been far from ideal parents. We've blown our tempers; we've misjudged you; we haven't always handled you wisely—and that's been tough on you. We get intense and overzealous, overpicky on some issues, and we completely overlook other issues. We're just plain ol' dumb human beings. But our goofs have an influence on how you turn out—that's the scary part."

Ray said, "We think you're just turning out great. But whatever scars you've got, they're our fault, not yours. And don't think we don't realize that."

"That's okay," said Nels. "I think you're great."

"We sure are crazy about you, Nels," I said.

"We're so proud of you," Ray added. "You're terrific—in spite of us."

"You're great parents," said Nels.

Over the seats of the car there were pats and smiles and squeezes.

That was it—and pretty soon we drove down the hill and home again.

52

Remember the illustration of the dog?—

When a dog finally realizes it can't win a fight, it shows its submission and surrender at the onset by lying down at the great dog's feet and baring its vulnerable throat and belly. In this position it could get killed in an instant. . . .

And that's how the dog is spared.

And that's how *you're* spared—before God. If you really want a fresh chance to begin again. . . .

And that's how you're spared before your family. Will you expose yourself? Will you risk getting "killed"?

A Project for You

Are you a childless couple, or a couple with children too young to be apologized to? Make a date for the two of you, in a tender setting. And:

Confess your sins to each other and pray for each other
so that you may be healed. The prayer of a righteous man
is powerful and effective.

James 5:16 (italics mine)

*If you have both adults and understanding children under
your roof, have a family meeting as soon as possible.*

1. First, father and mother need to apologize to each other
    before the children for their failures and lacks in communi-
    cation. Follow this with hugs and prayer for each other,
    with assurances of total forgiveness.

2. Then parents (or the single parent) need to apologize to the
    children. Tell them that you are responsible for much of
    what they are, including their weaknesses. Tell them you're
    sorry, and that you're willing to help solve some of the
    problems and get a fresh start. Stoop low. Let it be the
    beginning of the lift-up approach in your home.

3. Then as a family, kneel before God in prayer, holding
    hands. Let the parents lead the way in apologizing to God.
    Allow the children to do so also—if they want—but don't
    force. Pray encouragingly and in a lifting way for each child
    by name. Then lots of hugs!

    You're all wet cement together. From now on let God's
    Word and prayer impress you all, regularly, repeatedly.
    Into the storage boxes! (Remember your subconscious?)
    And let your love for each other impress you all, regularly,
    repeatedly. Could you get up a family project of a hug
    apiece once a day, or saying "I love you" once a day?

    Let it be *new beginning time.*

Epilogue

Here's a little section of some notes I took once when Ray was preaching a communion sermon. Let the words apply to your family, or to your relationship with your young friends:

Our being "broken bread" doesn't mean our being divided into separate pieces, like the disciples at Jesus' arrest who scattered and fled.

It means being like Jesus' own body: broken but whole. We're one in our brokenness; we're together in it.

Indeed, it's our brokenness which binds us together and makes us experientially one.

And that's how the fathers keep their hearts turned toward their children, and that's how the children keep their hearts turned toward their fathers.

That's what this book was trying to say to you. It led you through affirmations for newborns and little children, during the period when they can't possibly know your attitude toward yourself. It led you to the era around their twelfth birthday, when your affirmations are as strong as ever, but when your humility is also showing: "I have to begin to release you, my child, because I'm only a temporary guide for you. I'll be backing off soon, to let God take over. Then you'll be in perfect hands forever!"

And, oh, keep continually sinking into the deepest, sweetest, best way of all. Become like a little child, and lift up those around you. Let there be no more masking, posturing, faking on your part. Take the lowest place, where you're not trying to prove anything about yourself, you're only proving the others' great worth. Soon you'll find that the others have quit masking, posturing, and faking—and they're affirming *your* great worth! You *do* have great worth, and so do they, but each must discover and affirm the other's.

Through being continually broken, and continually affirming one another, the generations meet each other's needs, and minister to each other. And revival, renewal, becomes your constant, ever-fresh way of life.

The wet cement of immaturity then somehow becomes the mystical, continually broken cement of maturity. And in heaven we'll discover that what seemed broken to us was God's beautiful, smooth pavement to wholeness, unity, and completion.

Friend, I'm the one who wrote this book, but I need it more than you do. From this last page and onward, let's covenant together to live by affirmations ("I love you") and by confessions ("I'm sorry").

Right now let's go to Him together about it.

Lord Jesus, we accept as Your free gift the offer of Your affirming love and Your humility for our lives, so that the hearts of the older and younger generations may be kept turned toward each other in great tenderness and compassion.

Lord Jesus, we're ready for You. You can come at any time.

Anne Ortlund's hymn "Macedonia," included in many hardback hymnals today, was chosen as the theme hymn of Billy Graham's World Congress on Evangelism in Berlin.

Her books include:

- *Disciplines of the Beautiful Woman*
- *Disciplines of the Heart*
- *Disciplines of the Home*
  (these three now combined in *The Gentle Ways of the Beautiful Woman*)
- *Children Are Wet Cement*
- *Building a Great Marriage*
- *Love Me With Stubborn Love* (how-to's for small groups)
- *In His Presence*
- *Fix Your Eyes on Jesus*
- *Up with Worship* (newly republished, revised and updated)
- *My Sacrifice, His Fire* (weekday devotions for women)

With her husband:

- *A Fresh Start for Your Friendships*
- *Lord, Make My Life a Miracle* (newly republished, revised and updated)
- *You Don't Have to Quit*
- *How Great Our Joy* (Christmas gift book)

Ray and Anne can be reached at:

Renewal Ministries
4500 Campus Drive, Suite 662
Newport Beach, CA 92660
(949) 756-1313
Fax: (949) 756-1566
www.Ortlund.org

AUTHORS GUILD BACKINPRINT.COM EDITIONS are fiction and nonfiction works that were originally brought to the reading public by established United States publishers but have fallen out of print. The economics of traditional publishing methods force tens of thousands of works out of print each year, eventually claiming many, if not most, award-winning and one-time best-selling titles. With improvements in print-on-demand technology, authors and their estates, in cooperation with the Authors Guild, are making some of these works available again to readers in quality paperback editions. Authors Guild Backinprint.com Editions may be found at nearly all online bookstores and are also available from traditional booksellers. For further information or to purchase any Backinprint.com title please visit www.backinprint.com.

Except as noted on their copyright pages, Authors Guild Backinprint.com Editions are presented in their original form. Some authors have chosen to revise or update their works with new information. The Authors Guild is not the editor or publisher of these works and is not responsible for any of the content of these editions.

THE AUTHORS GUILD is the nation's largest society of published book authors. Since 1912 it has been the leading writers' advocate for fair compensation, effective copyright protection, and free expression. Further information is available at www.authorsguild.org.

Please direct inquiries about the Authors Guild and Backinprint.com Editions to the Authors Guild offices in New York City, or e-mail staff@backinprint.com.

0-595-22663-9